MERSEY MINIS

VOLUME TWO

LIVING

edited by

Deborah Mulhearn

Mersey Minis

VOLUME TWO: LIVING

Edited by Deborah Mulhearn
Illustrations by Clare Curtis
Graphic design by Ken Ashcroft
Printed and bound in Italy by Graphicom

ISBN: 978-0-9548431-8-2

First published in June 2007 by Capsica Ltd
83 Ampthill Road, Liverpool L17 9QN, UK

email: merseyminis@capsica.net
www.merseyminis.com
www.loveliverpoolbooks.com

CONTENTS

Dedicated to
Eva Helena Mulhearn

INTRODUCTION

LIVING is the second volume of Mersey Minis, a series of small books celebrating Liverpool's 800th anniversary. LIVING continues where the first volume, LANDING, left off. While LANDING looked at people's first impressions, LIVING reflects more of the life of the city and its environs. Beyond the choppy river and the massive dock walls, visitors are finding their feet and starting to explore this 'best built town'.

Americans at leisure, immigrants looking for lodgings, newcomers looking for adventure or acceptance, these evocative accounts capture the sights, sounds, smells and psyche of the bustling, bemusing and sometimes scary big city. Many are talking about the Liverpool of old, but their accounts are strikingly modern. They do the same as tourists and visitors do today. They compare and contrast. They stare in amazement and admiration at the huge dray horses, the strange modes of transport, the elegant shops, the new parks, the gin palaces and grog shops, even the Liverpudlian fashion sense! And they gripe, in time-honoured fashion, about the chilly weather, the soot-grimed stone, the 'frowning' buildings and the fog.

Some early visitors were almost certainly indulging in a little industrial espionage, checking out the new docks. Another 19th century traveller enquires about the city's emblem, the Liver Bird, long before the Liver Building graced the waterfront, and is answered in typically gnomic fashion.

LIVING also looks at the working and domestic life of the city. From dancing to the dole, shopping and strife, tower blocks and tunnels, LIVING has high life and low life and everything in between.

Some of these extracts have been unearthed from obscure journals and memoirs, bringing back to life long-forgotten layers of the city and its business. The biographies at the back of LIVING are necessarily short, but they reveal a little bit more about these extraordinary – and ordinary – lives, and along with the book list will hopefully prompt further reading.

DEBORAH MULHEARN

A NOTE ON THE TEXT

The extracts in Mersey Minis are reproduced from original sources, many of which are historic and therefore sometimes using styles and language unfamiliar to modern readers. I have, however, in most cases retained the original spellings, punctuation and sometimes the grammatical mistakes so as not to impede the energy and flow of the writer, and to reflect the uniqueness and idiosyncracy of his or her account.

The date given at the start of each extract is the date the writing refers to, and not necessarily when it was written or published. For publication dates and further details please see the book list on p109.

LIVING

John Brophy 1944

Fog, rain, pavements and gutters brown with mud, as if cold soup had been spilled lavishly over them: these were his memories of Liverpool, dimmed but not obliterated by the passage of time, till they revived now in the July sunshine in front of St George's Hall. Often the winter weather exceeded its own standard miseries. There would be snow and ice and sleet; thaw and frost again: gales that blustered deafeningly across the roof-tops and hurtled, with a cold edge like a knife, round street corners. What else made up his remembered picture of Liverpool for most of the year? Hot oily smells from the opening and closing doors of fried-fish shops. Great glass vases filled with dyed water, red, blue, green, yellow (the brightest colours of the Liverpool winter) all translucent from the lights behind them as they stood on the high shelves of chemists' windows. Booming melancholy signals which reverberated, unlocatable, all over the city, on days and nights of fog, from the sirens of ships in the river. The 'one o'clock gun', fired from Birkenhead, the Merseyside time signal, with its double or triple echoes high in the sky, and men stopping in the streets to check the accuracy of their watches. Boys in their early teens emerging from herbalist shops, their stomachs full of sarsaparilla, and with cigarettes made from lavender leaves stuck defiantly in their mouths. Slate-slabbed lavatories in side-streets, eternally stinking. Seamen of all nationalities plodding the pavements, Chinese, Lascars, Indians and Negroes the easiest to identify; babies, pushed about by brothers or sisters a few years older, in perambulators made from wooden soap-boxes. Men, out of work, leaning for hours on end against brick walls or standing, blank-faced, on the edge of the pavement; women with dirty shawls wound over shoulders and breast and half-concealing jugs of beer under the shawl-ends. And everyone, rich or poor, with their outer clothes perma-nently sodden from the winter damps. This was the Liverpool he remembered, and again he was thankful it belonged in the past.

Caroline Kirkland 1848

April 26th. We have spent two days in running about Liverpool, never weary of staring at the life, and manners, and customs, houses, and equipages, of a foreign people. To us, everything is new, strange, and exciting. The very color of the city, largely made of stone, originally soft in hue, but mellowed by smoke and rain, is full of charm for our eyes.

The style of building, reminding us most of Philadelphia, is essentially peculiar. It is massive, thorough, and to our inexpert ken, picturesque. The public buildings are substantial and costly, and the new Law building, not quite completed, is, on the whole, the most splendid edifice we have ever seen. We wonder that travellers have usually passed Liverpool by so contemptuously! We think an unsophisticated American, with an eye for what is characteristic, finds there a little of everything peculiar in English civilization; and we are not ashamed to own that we were kept staring with surprise and delight, or with painful interest and sad curiosity, during every moment of the day. Even to watch the endless variety of the carriages and carts; to see the huge drayhorses, more like elephants than horses; the beggars in the streets; the soldiers; the police; or to notice the 'strong' boots and shoes at the shop windows, was occupation exciting and amusing enough! If to these we add our first view of those gates of death, styled 'gin palaces', which make the windows of apothecaries pale with their gaudy splendor, and furnish by far the most striking features in a night view of the streets of Liverpool, we shall indicate the chief source of our interest at the first blush.

Paul Morley   2007

Liverpool is not part of England in the way that New York is not part of America. It is more Welsh, more Irish, a shifty, shifting outpost of defiance and determination reluctantly connected to the English mainland, more an island set in a sea of dreams and nightmares that's forever taking shape in the imagination, more a mysterious place jutting out into time between the practical, stabilising pull of history and the sweeping, shuffling force of myth.

William Cullen Bryant   1845

'Liverpool,' said one of its inhabitants to me, 'is more like an American than an English city; it is new, bustling, and prosperous.' I saw some evidences of this after I had got my baggage through the custom-house, which was attended with considerable delay, the officers prying very closely into the contents of certain packages which I was taking for friends of mine to their friends in England, cutting the packthread, breaking the seals, and tearing the wrappers without mercy. I saw the streets crowded with huge drays, carrying merchandise to and fro, and admired the solid construction of the docks, in which lay thousands of vessels from all parts of the globe. The walls of these docks are built of large blocks of red sandstone, with broad gateways opening to the river Mersey, and when the tide is at its height, which I believe is about thirty feet from low water, the gates are open, and vessels allowed to enter and depart. When the tide begins to retire, the gates are closed, and the water and the vessels locked in together. Along the river for miles, the banks are flanked with this massive masonry, which in some places I should judge to be nearly forty feet in height. Meantime the town is spreading into the interior; new streets are opened; in one field you may see the brickmakers occupied in their calling, and in the opposite one the bricklayers building rows of houses. New churches and new public buildings of various kinds are going up in these neighborhoods.

Reverend John Wesley   1755

At six in the morning, Tuesday, 15th, I preached to a large

and serious congregation; and then went on to Liverpool, one of the neatest, best built towns I have seen in England: I think it is full twice as large as Chester; most of the streets are quite straight. Two-thirds of the town, we were informed, have been added within these forty years. If it continues to increase in the same proportion, in forty years more it will nearly equal Bristol. The people, in general, are the most mild and courteous I ever saw in a sea-port town; as indeed appears by their friendly behaviour, not only to the Jews and Papists who live among them, but even to the Methodists (so called.) The preaching-house is a little larger than that at Newcastle. It was thoroughly filled at seven in the evening; and the hearts of the whole congregation seemed to be moved before the Lord, and before the presence of his power.

Margaret Simey   1999

The magic of Liverpool is that it isn't England. We are global and we have learned to tolerate and respect each other's traditions. As such, we are a national asset.

Samuel Sidney   1851

The best part of the town may be seen in a walk from St Luke's Church at the top of Bold Street, a short distance from the Adelphi Hotel, through Church Street, Lord Street, crossing Castle Street, down to St George's Pier. By this line the best and the busiest streets of Liverpool will be seen, with shops nearly equal to the finest in London, and with customers in fine ladies, who are quite as pretty, and much more finely dressed, than the residents of that paradise of provincial belles, Belgravia. Indeed both sexes in this town are remarkable for their good looks and fashionable costume, forming a strong contrast to the more busy inhabitants of Manchester.

In Bold Street is the Palatine, a miniature copy of the Clubs of Pall Mall: at the doors and windows may be seen, 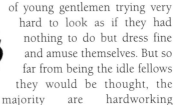 in the intervals of business, a number of young gentlemen trying very hard to look as if they had nothing to do but dress fine and amuse themselves. But so far from being the idle fellows they would be thought, the majority are hardworking merchants and pains-taking attorneys, who bet a little, play a little, dote upon a lord, and fancy that by being excessively supercilious in the *rococo* style of that poor heathen bankrupt Brummel, they are performing to perfection the character of men of fashion. This, the normal state of young Liverpool, at a certain period the butterfly becomes a grub, a money grub, and abandoning brilliant cravats, primrose gloves, and tight shiny boots, subsides into the respectable heavy father of genteel comedy, becomes a churchwarden, a patron of charities, a capitalist, and a highly respectable member of society.

Willy Russell   2001

There is something absolutely particular about Liverpool because of the nature of the idiom here. It is a wonderful language for someone who works in the spoken form.

George Head

I would recommend any grumbling discontented person to pay a visit to Liverpool, merely for the purpose of witnessing a specimen of the art of living well and cheap, as regards the very important affair of dinner. There, chance led me on one particular occasion to Keels's Hotel, which is, I think, in the large street leading from the Mansion House to St. George's Dock; however, at all events, it is what is called highly respectable, both as to its position and elevation. Having mistaken the hour of departure of one of the boats, I was directed hither by the policeman, who, to his recommendation, added in an awful cadence, that 'the magistrates themselves very often dined there.'

When I entered the coffee-room, nearly a score of people were seated at different tables, some with their hats off, others with their hats on, but all busily eating their dinner, and a chair and a table were provided for myself by a good-looking and very smartly dressed young woman, who officiated as

waiter. Constant communication was held with the bar at the head of the room, at which three or four other females presided. Upon inquiring what I could have for dinner, the young lady produced the *carte*, whence it appeared that there really was everything that an Englishman could possibly desire, in the matter of roasted and boiled meats, meat pies, and pastry. Neither was the adage, 'bis dat qui cito dat,' within these walls forgotten, for here a hungry man has no sooner made his selection, than in half a minute the smoke of the dish is actually curling under his nose. I think I never partook of a more glorious round of beef than that of which a plateful was now placed before me, together with a delicate lily-white heart of a young cabbage. Next came a delightful apple dumpling well sugared, the fruit transparent, and the crust excellent. The garniture of the table was homely but clean, the dishes and covers of queen's metal, as highly polished as silver. And after having eaten a sufficient quantity to satisfy any reasonable appetite, the charge for the whole was only one shilling. To conclude – I asked a gentleman sitting at an adjoining table how much it was customary to give the waiter, to which he replied, with a look of surprise, – nothing. Had I not come to the same conclusion long before, I certainly should have arrived at it now, namely, that so long as a man can procure so very good a dinner for a shilling, and be waited upon by a tidy young woman into the bargain, England cannot be, in spite of a vast deal of modern philosophy, so very bad a country to live in.

The young person referred to was really the pink of her profession, her movements being quiet, quick, dexterous, and I may add, graceful in a great degree. With no one to assist her, she waited upon not less than a score of people, who were no sooner satisfied than they went away, and were replaced by others; so that the whole set were nearly changed twice over during the half hour I remained in the room. Her eyes were in every corner at the same moment, so that every guest found his wants attended to, as soon almost as he was aware of them himself. At all events she was in perpetual motion, dropping a fork to one, a piece of bread to another, craving pardon of a third, as she reached across the table for a huge mug, and in the attitude of a flying Mercury, exposed precisely as much as was decent and proper of a well turned leg, and then away she would go to another quarter, wriggling about, in a way of her own, or in the French style, as if her feet were tied together, like a figure on wheels wound up by clock-work. Such an active being surely never could be still, – even in her sleep.

Shirley Hughes   c1940

Shop windows were a potent kind of theatre, especially the big Liverpool stores when they were all lighted up on a winter evening. The mannequins, poised with their careful Marcel waves and Cupid's bow mouths, seemed only to be waiting for a moment when nobody was watching to begin their nocturnal dance. Inside, the cosmetic-scented smell, bright showcases, sweeping staircases and escalators gave you a powerful sense of theatricality. Money taken at the counter was put into a capsule and whizzed on a wire up to a lady cashier who sat high up in a glass box like an exhibit. She inserted the receipt and the right change and sent it whizzing back. In the fabric department assistants handled the rolls of rayons, cottons, cretonnes and tweeds like conjurors; flourishing their big scissors, measuring, cutting the lengths exactly, folding and packing them into smart paper parcels. During the Liverpool blitz one of the sights which most brought home to me the sense of wanton destruction were those bolts of material, spilling out of a store which had been bombed and gutted overnight, flung into the sodden street amongst the splintered glass.

Samuel Taylor Coleridge   1812

The Liverpool Exchange & Custom House are noble Buildings, far surpassing those of London; but so miserable are the streets with one exception, that of the High Street which terminates in these grand Erections, that the whole presented to my fancy the thought of a magnificent Palace rising out of a vast dunghill with one broad clean road made thro' the dung straight up to it.

Edward Patey   1967

Half a century ago, two cathedrals in such close proximity would have been interpreted in terms of ecclesiastical rivalry. Today, at both ends of Hope Street, we rejoice at the new ecumenical spirit which has rightly been described as the great new fact of our era.

Gerard Manley Hopkins   1889

Next spitting in the North of England is very, very common

with the lower classes: as I went up Brunswick Road (or any street) at Liverpool on a frosty morning it used to disgust me to see the pavement regularly starred with the spit of the workmen going to their work; and they do not turn aside, but spit straight before them as you approach, as a Frenchman remarked to me with abhorrence and I cd. only blush.

Charles Nevin   2004

Liverpool. People, I think it's fair to say, tend to have an opinion about Liverpool. And it's also fair to say, I think, that these opinions are not always entirely positive. Let me attempt a description of the physical reaction I have most often encountered, particularly among the metropolitan middle classes, at the sound of that name: a rapid progress from curled lip to raised eyes to deep sigh. Try it yourself on one of them and see what I mean.

And then, depending on articulacy, intelligence, the time of day and the ingestion of artificial stimulants, they will be off, flat out, in top sneer, on a tour de Scouse that will take in the dreadful accent, the awful tracksuits, how they all think they're so bloody funny and how you call one in a tie the defendant, how they're always whinging and never working, and always blaming everybody else for everything, old Boris Johnson and *The Spectator* were absolutely bloody right to call them peculiar, deeply unattractive and all the rest of it. Remarkable.

Thomas Patten   1697

I am informed that there is a design to bring a bill into the

House of Commons against fish wears that hinder navigation, in navigable rivers, and that take and destroy fish and the fry of fish. You very well know the mischief that is done in the River Mersey or at least heard that vast numbers of salmon-trout are taken, so as to supply all the county and market towns twenty miles around; and when the county is cloyed, or when they cannot get sale for them, they give them to the swine. Your brother did formally take three or four salmon a week at a fishing, in or near Speke, but, of late, hath taken very few, or none, of which he hath complained to me; and he imputed this loss to the destruction of the fry, and hath after threatened to prosecute your fishermen.

Then again these wears are as mischievous another way, by their hindering the passage of ships, boats and barges; as for example, in the same River Mersey what a vast advantage would be to Liverpool if the river were made navigable to Manchester and Stockport. Since I made it navigable to Warrington there had been sent to Liverpool, and from Liverpool, 2,000 tons of goods a year, and I believe, as much by land, which if the river were cleaned of wears, would all go by water, for the river to Manchester is very capable of being made navigable at a very small charge. And this would encourage all tradesmen in Manchester, Stockport, Macclesfield, Congleton, Bolton, Bury, Rochdale, some parts of Yorkshire, Derbyshire and Stafford to come to Liverpool and buy their goods instead of going to London; the carriage would be so easy and cheap it would nearly double the trade of Liverpool.

Walter Dixon Scott 1907

And then one would like to appraise the elusive atmosphere of Bold Street – that intimate, elegant avenue of rare fabrics and shopping women and the ripe, drumming ripple of automobiles – the Bond Street of Liverpool, whose wood pavements make a sudden chosen silence in the midst of the clatter, which is held beautifully inviolate from electric cars and sandwichmen, and at the head of whose discreet vista the tower of St Luke's rises gravely up, faintly remindful of the manner in which the towers of Sainte Gudule survey that other road of women and priceless elegancies in Brussels.

Edward Lucie-Smith 1967

A man trying to write poetry in Liverpool usually has the attitudes of a frontiersman: life is harder, but in some ways cleaner and better.

Johann Georg Kohl 1844

Among the great cities of the world, of first or second rank, there is no other so exclusively devoted to commerce. Every house in Liverpool is either a counting-house, a warehouse, a shop, or a house that in one way or other is either an instrument or the result of trade. The great buildings and institutions of the town are a custom-house, an exchange, a set of docks, a railway station, or something else that is intended, directly or indirectly, to be serviceable to commerce, and the inhabitants are nearly to a man traders or the servants of traders.

George Henry Heffner 1876

Traveling-bag in hand, which contained my entire wardrobe, I now went in search of an hotel. The 'Angel Hotel' was soon pointed out to me, and on entering it, I learned that several of my fellow-passengers had already taken rooms there. It is entirely under the control of ladies, being managed by a proprietress and female clerks. The house is an excellent one, and the accommodations are first-class. It bears a very appropriate name. After partaking of a hardy supper, I walked out to 'take a look at Europe!' At 6:45 p.m., I entered St. Peter's Church, and was conducted to a pew. Here, as elsewhere in Europe, the young and the old of both sexes occupy the same seat together. One of the little boys of the family occupying the same pew with me, gave me a hymn-book. A part of the exercises consisted in chanting psalms. The eagle lectant and the Bible characters represented in the stained glass of the windows soon enlisted my attention, but the meaning of having two birds perched upon a high stand in the middle of the church, I could not unfold, nor was there any one about that could tell me. The next day I saw the same bird beside a noble female form in the museum. 'What bird is that?' said I to a by-stander. 'That figure,' said he, 'is the emblem of Liverpool, and the bird is the *liver*, which abounded down in the pools, and after which the place was first named.'

Roger McGough 2000

You won't find me under M for McGough, you have to look under L for Liverpool poets. We were seen as interesting sociologically, but nothing to do with English Literature. I've even had people say to me: it's all right for you – you were born in Liverpool, as if that made me automatically poetic.

Christopher Colbeck   1831

Having given as much information as I could collect I have now only to resume my narrative from the finishing of my rail conveyance, but the mouth of the tunnel being three-quarters of a mile from the busy part of the town, conveyances of all descriptions are hired to drop the passengers at their homes. So jumped in an omnibus and was dropped in Brunswick Street where, espying a very neat hotel, I sojourned there having had tea and during its preparation had a comfortable change. On finishing my meal I strolled first to St. James Cemetery which is laid out in walks and shrubberies which a few are buried on the Grass Flat, a part of which is apportioned for the Monument to the memory of Huskisson who lies buried here. The ground is excavated and is stone of very hard quality. A number of Avenues lead to the different Vaults.

From the cemetery I went on St. James Terrace from which you have a very excellent view of the Town, Docks, River and the Cheshire Coast opposite. I then strolled back to the Town which is exceeding handsome and the Houses are built in a substantial manner. Lord St. is about the principal for trade and Piccadilly where they have some buildings arranged similar to the London 'Regent Circus'. It was at a house here I was attracted by an Organ playing and observing it to be a Museum I went all over the house. It was but a poor collection of stuffed Birds, Beasts, Serpents etc. with a man playing a very excellent toned Organ. I then went to the exchange, a Quadrangle of magnificent buildings in the centre of which is a superbly executed monument to the memory of Lord Nelson. I then being invited by the Play Bills adjourned to the Theatre where I had the pleasure of seeing Mrs W. West and hearing Mr Sinclair in Masaniello. The Playhouse was neither so large or tastefully decorated as I expected and the attendance but very thin. The performances were over by half past 11 and I then enjoyed a ramble through two or three Markets splendidly lit up with Gas and altogether of a first rate character. I now managed to find my way to Brunswick St. and having slightly refreshed myself went to Bed.

Eleanor Rathbone   c1820

It was the custom then for prosperous men of business to live as William Rathbone's father and grandfather did, opposite to or above their own offices and warehouses, and on fine evenings they took the air sitting by the dockside, while their children played at a safe distance from the deep water. St Anne's Street was then the fashionable abode of the great West Indian merchants of the day, while Rodney Street was the new quarter to which some of them, including Mr Gladstone's father, had migrated.

J B Priestley   1933

I have never been near Liverpool in spring, summer and early autumn. My visits have all been wintry. I find it impossible to imagine what the city looks like in clear bright sunshine. I think of it existing in a shortened year, only running from November to February, with all its citizens for ever wearing thick overcoats. Just before you reach Lime Street Station your train runs into a deep cutting and daylight promptly vanishes, never returning, I feel, until your other homeward train has left Lime Street and Liverpool well behind. It has, in my memory, more fog about than other cities, not excepting London. The centre is imposing, dignified and darkish, like a city in a rather gloomy Victorian novel. Does spring ever arrive in St. John's Gardens? Do the birds ever twitter and flutter before the solemn façade of St. George's Hall? Is there a Mersey, so much green flowing water, not simply a misty nothingness hooting dismally? I must go there in June, some time, to find out.

There was no deep dark railway cutting for me on this occasion, for I arrived by road, and in place of the cutting were streets that went on and on and on through dreary regions infested by corporation trams. The surface of these streets was a slippery abomination; though we were going very slowly, three times we were nearly on top of pedestrians who started up not three yards from our radiator and slithered

about as if bent on suicide. When I was able to think, I began to gather together what I knew already about Liverpool and remembered what I could of previous visits. Well, there was the Playhouse, and its director, my friend William Armstrong, who considers himself – probably with some truth – the busiest man in the city, for he is always watching one play, producing another, and making plans for the production of two more. His, I suppose, is the best repertory company in the kingdom; no other, except perhaps Birmingham in its heyday, has sent so many brilliant young actors and actresses to the West End; but I decided there was no room in this chronicle for William and the Playhouse. On two previous visits I had been given a dinner at the University Club. A very jolly little club it is too, where they know how to turn Liverpool winter into something like summer, at least for one evening: pleasant journalists, with Mr. Macleay, of the *Liverpool Daily Post*, at the head of them; smiling professors and their ladies; young barristers and shipping men: all very good company and as hospitable as you please. Let me admit that their Liverpool exists, and does it admirably. But it was not the Liverpool I wanted now. The surgeons in Rodney Street (where Gladstone was born), with its fine late eighteenth-century fronts? The Cathedral, which remained in my memory as a vast dark-red bulk, immensely impressive but tantalising because it just missed being a noble expression of our own age? The great buildings down by the river, such as the Dock Board Offices, the Cunard and Royal Liver palaces? Unusual for England – as if Liverpool had had so many peeps at New York's water-front that it felt it must do *something* – but not material for me. What else was there? Birkenhead, where the middle-class folk have comfortably established themselves in villas on the hill? I had had a lunch and tea or two over there, in solid Victorian comfort, but this time I wanted to see something quite different. The cotton brokers and the shipping men? I had met both kinds, and no doubt they would have a lot to say to me – and what they would say would be well worth hearing – if I met some of them again. They were genuine Liverpool, I admitted to myself, but even they did not fit into this mysterious composition that so far was purely negative. I had very little time; the whole of Lancashire was waiting, and there was my new play to attend to in Manchester at the week-end, for it was opening there; so what was it I wanted? We had now arrived in the heart of the big city, and as usual it was almost a heart of darkness. But it looked like a big city, there was no denying that. Here, emphatically, was the English seaport second only to London. The very weight of stone emphasised that fact. And even if the sun never seems to rise properly over it, I like a big city to proclaim itself a big city at once. If it must have a thousand Corporation trams lumbering and screeching and groaning about the place, let it build up and up, as Liverpool has done, to dwarf the mournful beasts. We had cut and curved our way to the very entrance, the imposing entrance, of the Adelphi Hotel. I believe that the Adelphi was originally built for the first-class Atlantic passenger traffic, and unfortunately for Liverpool and its luxury hotel, that traffic was immediately afterwards diverted to Southampton; with the result that the Adelphi has been hot from mingled shame and vexation ever since, rather too hot for my comfort, even in the dead winter of Liverpool. But there I was, signing my name in the register, and as yet I had no programme of exploration. There was a Liverpool I wanted for this book, and I had still to decide which it was. But I know it was something quite unlike the interior of the Adelphi, which is an hotel that no producer of musical comedy would object to using for his big set in the Second Act. What was it then? Up in my bedroom I reminded myself that it was

 probably Liverpool the seaport that contained what I wanted. I had been to Southampton and Bristol; I was on my way to the Tyne and Hull; but there was something here that none of these ports could show me. The search was narrowing.

I began telephoning to one or two newspaper acquaintances in the city. I was on the trail.

Howard Gayle   1977

I'd always wondered why players from inner city areas like Toxteth weren't being given the chance or making the grade, even before I played with Liverpool. People from our area were looked upon as troublesome. The clubs said at the time that they hadn't spotted any talent. I was fortunate that I was playing for a Sunday league team and the manager Eric Dunlop knew a scout at Liverpool and he pestered and pestered him and eventually I got asked for a trial. They must have known I was black because he was known for multi-racial teams. I thought I had broken the mould but I was forever shouting about it because there were better players than me around who didn't get the opportunity. There'd only been one black player at Everton, Cliff Marshall, and it was widely publicised about the racial abuse he was receiving, so maybe young black players didn't relish the thought of going into the clubs.

Nathaniel Hawthorne   1853

I don't know any place that brings all classes into contiguity on equal ground so completely as the waiting-room at Rock Ferry on these frosty days. The room is not more than eight feet square, with walls of stone, and wooden benches ranged round them, and an open stove in one corner, generally well furnished with coal. It is almost always crowded, and I rather suspect that many persons who have no fireside elsewhere creep in here and spend the most comfortable part of their day.

This morning, when I looked into the room, there were one or two gentlemen and other respectable persons; but in the best place, close to the fire, and crouching almost into it, was an elderly beggar, with the raggedest of overcoats, two great rents in the shoulders of it disclosing the dingy lining, all bepatched with various stuff covered with dirt, and on his shoes and trousers the mud of an interminable pilgrimage. Owing to the posture in which he sat, I could not see his face, but only the battered crown and rim of the very shabbiest hat that ever was worn. Regardless of the presence of women (which, indeed, Englishmen seldom do regard when they wish to smoke), he was smoking a pipe of vile tobacco; but, after all, this was fortunate, because the man himself was not personally fragrant. He was terribly squalid, – terribly; and when I had a glimpse of his face, it well befitted the rest of his development, – grizzled, wrinkled, weather-beaten, yet sallow, and down-looking, with a watchful kind of eye,

turning upon everybody and everything, meeting the glances of other people rather boldly, yet soon shrinking away; a long thin nose, a gray beard of a week's growth; hair not much mixed with gray, but rusty and lifeless; – a miserable object; but it was curious to see how he was not ashamed of himself, but seemed to feel that he was one of the estates of the kingdom, and had as much right to live as other men. He did just as he pleased, took the best place by the fire, nor would have cared though a nobleman were forced to stand aside for him. When the steamer's bell rang, he shouldered a large and heavy pack, like a pilgrim with his burden of sin, but certainly journeying to hell instead of heaven. On board he looked round for the best position, at first stationing himself near the boiler-pipe; but, finding the deck damp underfoot, he went to the cabin-door, and took his stand on the stairs, protected from the wind, but very incommodiously placed for those who wished to pass. All this was done without any bravado or forced impudence, but in the most quiet way, merely because he was seeking his own comfort, and considered that he had a right to seek it. It was an Englishman's spirit; but in our country, I imagine, a beggar considers himself a kind of outlaw, and would hardly assume the privileges of a man in any place of public resort. Here beggary is a system, and beggars are a numerous class, and make themselves, in a certain way, respected as such.

Isabella Blow   2002

Do you know, if you wear a flat heel in Liverpool, they think you're a lesbian?

Johann Georg Bodmer 1816

December 3 In the morning after breakfast I went to Mr. Rathbone who told one of his junior clerks to act as my guide. We saw the docks, two hemp roperies and a sugar refinery. Both the rope works were very good and produced ropes of excellent quality. An immense amount of capital must have been required to start these works. They could be used to make sailcloth. It seems to me however that the spinning of the hemp had not reached the highest state of perfection. Although the making of ropes was done in a very efficient manner I prefer the new methods used by Mr. Reyner in London. Reyner twists the rope on the spot as soon as it has been drawn through the tar. In this way the middle strands of the rope are drawn just as tightly together as the outer strands. Consequently the rope is much stronger than if it were made by hand.

I took a walk to my hotel so as to change before dining with Mr. Rathbone. I might add that I also saw an oil mill which resembles an oil press but I was unable to discover its purpose. After dinner I had no choice but to go to a concert which I did not find particularly elevating. What annoyed me most was that I have to agree to go to functions of this sort if I am to see what I want to see in a town. I went to bed at 1 a.m. only moderately satisfied with what I have done today.

December 4 I did some studying in the morning and then went to a ropery where I was delighted to have an opportunity of seeing a fine machine in action. Then I called on Mr. Camps – a Quaker recommended to me by Walduck – and he took me to the Botanic Garden. But the garden was either not open or the attendants had just gone to lunch. So we

went to see a windmill which was operated in a very efficient manner. I examined the works very thoroughly. I was particularly pleased with the way in which the grain was cleaned. All types of grain (without exception) were handled in this mill. I saw a special kind of drying process in action which dealt with the grain as it came from the millstones.

We were now able to get into the Botanic Garden which is really very beautiful. I greatly enjoyed my visit and I certainly enjoyed the fine greenhouse where plants from all over the world have been assembled. I was particularly interested in the plant called a 'fly catcher'. If one tickles this plant with a stick or a straw – or if a fly enters the aperture – the plant closes very quickly and very firmly and it remains closed until the fly is dead. I cannot help thinking for what wonderful purpose such a living plant should have been created.

I returned to my hotel from the Botanic Garden and continued with my studies and my drawings until midnight when I went to bed. I was by no means dissatisfied with what I had done today.

Jack Straw

You know what Scousers are like, they're always up to something. Please do not repeat that to anyone from Liverpool.

William Ewart Gladstone

c1815

Mr Rawson was a good man, of high no-popery opinions. His school afterwards rose into considerable repute, and it had Dean Stanley and the sons of one or more other Cheshire families for pupils. But I think this was not so much due to its intellectual stamina as to the extreme salubrity of the situation on the pure dry sands of the Mersey's mouth, with all the advantages of the strong tidal action and the fresh and frequent north-west winds. At five miles from Liverpool Exchange, the sands, delicious for riding, were one absolute solitude, and only one house looked down on them between us and the town.

Otto Frisch

1940

Things were more complicated when one summer night I was cycling home during curfew hours, having by then obtained permission to do so. I was stopped by a constable and was getting ready to explain my peculiar position; but all he was concerned about was that I was riding without lights. I assured him that it was still light enough to see, but he said that it was past lighting-up time and proceeded to take down my name and address. All the time I expected that at any moment he would spot my foreign name and accent and ask me 'What the devil are you doing here on a bicycle *and* after curfew?' But I was speaking my best English, and he probably took me for one of those Londoners who to a Liverpudlian anyhow sound like foreigners. So eventually I was allowed to go home, having turned on my lamps.

A couple of weeks later I received not one summons but two: one referring to my front lamp and one to my rear lamp! I rather fancied myself standing in Court and pleading my case, but unfortunately the summons was for a date right in the middle of a short holiday which I had planned to spend with the Peierlses in Cornwall. So I went to the police and asked what I should do and whether the date could be changed. No, the date could not be changed: but I was advised to write a personal note to the magistrate, pleading guilty and assuring him I wouldn't do it again. I was fined ten shillings, five for each lamp.

There were worse offences which I committed quite unwittingly. An old friend from Vienna, Dr Herz, a heart specialist who had been nicknamed the Herz-Herz (because Herz means heart in German) had settled in Wales, not very far from Liverpool, in the town of Mold. As  I was very fond of him, I went to visit him every few Sundays. I took a bus to Chester and usually spent a little time walking around that picturesque town with its old cloisters and its lovely cathedral, before catching another bus to Mold where I spent a pleasant afternoon with that wise old man. He had one oddity, perhaps from past times when he had many appointments to keep; he often wanted to know the exact time, and he carried two watches to make quite sure.

Coming back was sometimes more difficult; by the time I was on the bus from Chester to Liverpool the air-raid sirens had gone, and some bus drivers simply refused to drive into the bombardment. They stopped somewhere outside Liverpool and said 'Everybody get off, the bus doesn't go any further'. Then the only way to get home was to try and cadge a lift, and many a time have I entered Liverpool on top of an army lorry; an odd vehicle for an enemy alien to ride! Moreover I discovered after the war that Chester was like Liverpool, a prohibited area which enemy aliens were not allowed to enter, and a different one from Liverpool; so I ought to have had permission from two Chief Constables each time I undertook the journey! But I was never picked up; I didn't even know that I was breaking the law.

In the laboratory it took me a while to find where everything was, and Chadwick had thoughtfully allotted one of his students, John Holt, to help me. In those days I was an energetic, fast-moving fellow, and with the student usually trailing behind me I found that we had become nicknamed 'Frisch and Chips'. I hasten to add that 'Chips' has since become a full Professor in the University of Liverpool.

Lynette Arden   1974

When I went out with my camera subjects that would have been everyday and probably not particularly interesting to other Liverpool residents fascinated me because they were unfamiliar. Sometimes when people saw me in the streets they thought I was a reporter. I recall one woman stopping me and telling me I should visit her place to see what a bad state it was in. She may have thought that some publicity would get the authorities to act. The children I saw in the streets were lively, but the background they lived in seemed difficult.

I photographed children on their bikes in a street in Liverpool 8. Their faces struck me as being full of bravado and mischief. These children showed no trace of shyness; they were obviously ready to take on the world, whatever that might bring. Looking at the photos now they bring back the memories of Liverpool quite sharply. Black and white and gray seems to fit my images of these streets.

James Stonehouse   c1816

I recollect the bath-woman sold a sort of parliament cake, covered over with coloured sugar plums, and also some sweet things which in appearance resembled slugs. I never see these carraway-cakes and confections in the low shops in which they are now only sold, without thinking of the fat old bath-woman, who was a terror to me and others of my size and age. In 1816 these baths were discontinued and pulled down on the opening of George's Pier-head baths. For a mile or more there was good bathing on the shore. The bathing machines were introduced about the end of the last century. The keeper of the 'Wishing Gate-house' had several, and an old man who lived in a low hut near the mill (the remains of which still stand in the Waterloo-road) had two or three, and made money by them. At that time Bootle and Bootle Marshes were wild places, the roads execrable, and as for frogs (Bootle organs), the noise they made at night was wonderful. I recollect all the docks and streets from Bath-street downwards being sand-hills and salt-marshes. New Quay, of which Bath-street was a continuation, was a sort of haven, into which small vessels, at certain times of the tide, ran to discharge their cargoes. On the tide receding the vessels were left high and dry upon the bank. Bathers used to be seen in any number on the shore. Decency was so frequently outraged that the authorities were at last compelled to take steps to redress the grievance.

Matthew Arnold   1882

Money-making is not enough by itself. Industry is not enough by itself. Seriousness is not enough by itself. I speak now of the kinds of stimulus most in use with people of our race, and above all in business communities such as Liverpool. Respectable these kinds of stimulus may be, useful they may be, but they are not by themselves sufficient. The need in man for intellect and knowledge, his desire for beauty, his instinct for society, and for pleasurable and grace-ful forms of society, require to have their stimulus felt also, felt and satisfied. You know better than I can, how far adequate provision has hitherto been made in Liverpool for all this. But I imagine you are by no means satisfied with the sort of stimulus which the resources, pleasures, and amuse-ments of this great city, this port and passage place of the world, at present afford to your people, and above all to the young. You would own that the standard of life, as the polit-ical economists say, that the standard of life, in respect to these sources of stimulation, is at present pitched far too low. Well, in establishing this College you are on the way to raise it higher, to introduce a better balance of activities. You provide by this College a direct stimulus and satisfaction to the need in human nature for intellect and knowledge. But you at the same time provide indirectly a powerful help to the desire for beauty and to the social spirit. For intellectual culture quickens the wish for a proper satisfaction to these; and if by means of this College intellectual culture becomes a power among you, without doubt it will gradually affect and transform the amusements, pleasures, society, even the aspect and architecture, of Liverpool.

Bill Drummond 1976

Peter O'Hallaghan didn't look like a hippie, more a Scouse Beat. So he was OK with my prejudices of the time. I didn't really understand what he was on about but it resonated and I remembered it almost word for word, which is unusual for me. O'Hallaghan then told me he too had had a dream and in this dream he could see the spring bubbling forth from the cast-iron drain cover in the middle of the road where Button Street, Mathew Street and a couple of other roads met. The morning after his dream he came down to Mathew Street, and sure enough there was a manhole cover. He did some research at the library and discovered there was a spring there that had been covered in Victorian times and channelled into the city's sewerage system. On the corner of Mathew Street and Rainford Gardens was a warehouse with a 'To Let' sign. He went to the bank, got a loan, got the lease and was now setting up the Liverpool School of Language, Music, Dream and Pun. He had commissioned a bust of Jung which would be set in the outside wall of the building.

I jacked in my job building and painting stage sets at the Everyman Theatre and became a pupil of the school. Moved all my tools and my workbench into the basement of the warehouse. The ground floor was divided into market stalls under the name 'Aunt Twacky's', selling groovy tat, second-hand records and brown rice. On the first floor O'Hallaghan, his cousin Sean and a sculptor called Charles Alexander opened O'Hallaghan's Tea Room. It soon became the creative hub of the city. For the price of a mug of tea a generation of dole-queue dreamers spent their days discussing the poems they had written, the books they were writing, the happenings they were staging, the bands they were forming.

The people of Liverpool were proudly insular; none of my fellow pupils at the school sipping their mugs of tea gave a shit whether anybody in London ever heard of their existence or if any quarter of the media ever documented their creativity. All that mattered was what other people thought within the city state of Liverpool. Every day people staged impromptu performances, happenings, readings, installations, exhibitions, while Peter O'Hallaghan communicated his wisdom from behind the tea bar. Ken Campbell, the iconoclast of British theatre, arrived and decided it was the place to set up his Science Fiction Theatre of Liverpool. I was enlisted to design and build the sets for the company's premier production, a twelve-hour adaptation of the *Illuminatus* trilogy of books.

The rains were heavy. Late one night while I was hard at work building sets in the cellar, water began to seep through the walls. The seep grew to a gurgle. The gurgle to a flow. I was ankle deep and my bench began to float. The spring under the manhole cover must have been flooding. 'The sewers can't take it, captain.' The Pool of Life was coming to get me.

Daniel Clarke Eddy   1859

Perhaps the stranger's attention is arrested, in an English town, by nothing more than the heavy, massive, frowning appearance of the public and private buildings. The eye of an American, which has long gazed upon neat white dwellings and churches, enclosed in gardens of luxuriant freshness, soon tires with the dull monotony of a city all built of brick and stone, blackened by age and storms, and begrimed with the smoke of the chimney and the dust of the furnace. The buildings in Liverpool all look as if built to last through time. They seem to defy the heat of summer and the blasts of winter – the assaults of time, and the ravages of fire and sword. Among the churches is one of cast iron; and another for the blind, in which the singing is done by, and the congregation composed chiefly of, the poor, unfortunate inmates of the blind asylum, a charity which adorns the city of Liverpool even more than its docks, or its commercial advantages.

Hans Gál   1940

In Huyton we were received by a whole company, transferred to buses and delivered to our destination. We were led into a hut with long tables and benches and were given tea, bread and cheese, and a burly captain made a speech of welcome in which he appealed for our good behaviour. We shall be able to arrange our lives as we wish. Anyone who wants to can take part in 'digging for peace'. He paused slightly before the last word: the slogan 'digging for victory' evidently seemed to him to be tactless when addressing German prisoners. How difficult it must be to understand what a refugee is!! He doesn't look nasty, but his face is completely expressionless, with eyes like a pig's and bloated, blue cheeks, suggesting much whisky.

After this we were distributed into our quarters. We are the first occupants of this camp, which has apparently just been evacuated for receiving internees. We immediately formed ourselves into groups, in order to stay together. Ten to twelve men were assigned to each house, filled straw sacks were there, and we made ourselves as comfortable as we could manage in the dark, as there is no light, although electricity is installed.

Today we had a late breakfast – as the kitchens are not yet working properly – in the same mess hut in which we were received yesterday. There is a whole row of such huts behind the back of our road, and there are, as it now appears, all sorts of connecting roads all around that are still empty and blocked off. There will evidently be further arrivals. The breakfast was meagre, we would be glad now to get the despised porridge from the Donaldson Hospital, but we were assured that it would get better when everything was running smoothly. In the meantime we have nothing. The quickest thing to be organised was the kitchen detachment; there are many experts among us, and no-one will starve in the kitchen service.

I make a tour of the camp. On the far side of the mess hut is a piece of heath and behind it a little wood, but this is separated from our area by barbed wire; the soldiers parade there in the afternoons. Quite a way beyond that is the semi-circle of the houses of the village, which directly adjoins our camp at the other end – the left end of the T – and is separated from us only by the barbed-wire fence that limits our world. Inquisitive children stand there, no doubt puzzling over the strange people inside the cage. I must confess that we don't look nice. Most are unshaven, without ties, in a get-up in which one would, under normal circumstances, never have ventured out on to the street. The first mangy prison beards are beginning to sprout, unfortunately also on the cheeks of my room-mates. Schneider and Sugar have solemnly sworn not to shave in internment. I am curious to see how long they will keep it up.

Frederick Douglass   1845

The second day after my arrival at Liverpool, in company with my friend, Buffum, and several other friends, I went to Eaton Hall, the residence of the Marquis of Westminster, one of the most splendid buildings in England. On approaching the door, I found several of our American passengers, who came out with us in the *Cambria*, waiting for admission, as but one party was allowed in the house at a time. We all had to wait till the company within came out. And of all the faces, expressive of chagrin, those of the Americans were preëminent. They looked as sour as vinegar, and as bitter as gall, when they found I was to be admitted on equal terms with themselves. When the door was opened, I walked in, on an equal footing with my white fellow-citizens, and from all I could see, I had as much attention paid me by the servants that showed us through the house, as any with a paler skin. As I walked through the building, the statuary did not fall down, the pictures did not leap from their places, the doors did not refuse to open, and the servants did not say, '*We don't allow niggers in here!*'

Henry Stripe 1840

I was not sorry to leave the foundry in some respects for most of the hands working piece-work, the making up of the weekly wages was a long & laborious job. I scarcely ever got home on Friday evenings, it took me all the night reckoning the wages, as well as the following Saturday morning.

There were upwards of 150 boys employed cutting the threads on the screw bolts, securing chairs to the sleepers – each one having a separate screwing machine – everyone at piece work. These boys used so much oil in their operations that they became completely coated with it and waterproof.

One day a body of women came to ask Mr Maw to substitute something else in place of oil, for they paid when the poor children came near the fire of an evening to warm themselves, their smell became so offensive the parents had to leave the room.

After this Mr Maw substituted 'soft soap' instead.

William Enfield 1773

Few places enjoy a more healthful climate, or happy temperature of heat and cold, than Leverpool. It is screened from the severe easterly winds in the winter, by the range of high lands on that side; and the refreshing sea-breezes from the west, frequently allay the excessive heat of summer. Snow, which falls here but rarely, seldom lies long; nor indeed any where upon the sea coast. Frost is never so intense here as in the inland countries. In the hot and sultry months it seldom happens that the atmosphere is perfectly calm; the sea affording that perpetual current of air which is a circumstance of such great importance to the healthfulness of large and populous cities. The transitions from heat to cold, and from cold to heat, are indeed frequent and sudden; no place perhaps has a greater variety of weather. It must also be confessed, that the air in general is moister than in more elevated situations. Copious exhalations from the Irish sea, formed into low clouds, and carried along by the stream of air attending the flowing tides, frequently water the banks of the Dee and the Mersey without extending further; which may in part account for the common observation, that greater quantities of rain fall annually in the southern parts of Lancashire, than in most other parts of England.

This humidity of the atmosphere often occasions thick fogs and dark weather in the winter season; but is very serviceable in spring and summer, by affording a degree of moisture proper for vegetation to this sandy soil, which would otherwise quickly suffer by drought. The sea air renders the town so healthful, that, though it is exceedingly populous and closely built, epidemical disorders seldom appear, and when they do, are of short duration.

The effects of the winds upon the state of the weather is generally as follows. The north-west winds are turbulent and stormy; the southern productive of rain; the easterly winds often accompany a serene sky, and the severest cold and frost usually come with a north or north east wind.

The soil in and near Leverpool is dry and sandy for two miles round. The north shore consists of barren sands for an extent of twenty miles: but between the town and Kirkdale is a fine vale, which has a rich marle under the surface, and affords excellent pasturage. This tract of ground was formerly common arable land, but has been many years inclosed. The soil in the neighbourhood of this town is particularly favourable to the growth of potatoes; an article highly useful to the poor, acceptable to the rich, and profitable to the industrious farmer. The cultivation of this excellent root has of late been so much attended to in this county, that the husbandman often depends more upon a crop of potatoes than of wheat or any other grain.

Samuel Sullivan Cox 1851

Every object, even the go-carts, strike a stranger queerly at first. Omnibuses, with nobody inside, and crowded a-top, dash past our windows. Cabs as big as our carriages, like a streak of lightning, dash by with one horse. Horns musically quiver in the fresh morning air. The tall dark houses and clean white paves of Liverpool surround us, while on every side green foliage and twittering birds betoken that love of rural life which the English bring even into their cities. One thing in-doors is noticeable. The sedulous zeal displayed in curtaining out heaven's sun light. It would seem that, with the prodigality of gloomy weather in this isle, as much of the light as possible would be admitted, more especially as a heavy window tax is assessed. But no such thing. Why? Is it a phase of that habitual exclusiveness and love of domestic ease which form so prominent a trait in the English character?

We have viewed the city. Its Corinthian elegance of architecture, illustrated especially in the Exchange; excellent police; above all, its magnificent docks, by which the shipping is brought into the city and preserved afloat, notwithstanding the tides – bespeak for Liverpool the encomium of the traveller. There are two provisos. The first, beggars, I have named. The other is, the apparent sacriligious treatment of the buried dead. Would you believe it? The pave to several of the first churches here is over and upon the tombstones of the buried. The inscriptions are being effaced by the feet of the passenger. Nurses with children, men, women, and boys, indiscriminately, tread over the ashes of the departed.

George Garrett c1920

Unemployment spread. Black-coated professionals and small shopkeepers joined the parish queues. They had spent their last penny before applying for relief. Their pants were creased, they wore natty hats and carried raincoats over their arms. Holding themselves erect, they seldom spoke to anyone.

A few months 'queuing it' broke them down. Their shoulders drooped, their faces turned pale. Their pants became baggy, their bowler hats stained. But they were still reticent about speaking of themselves.

One had been a pianist before the war. After the armistice he toured the concert halls. Then the cinema forced the halls out of business. When the talkies came he couldn't even get a booking in the cinema. He sank into poverty, living with his wife and baby girl in one room. He was granted twenty-two shillings.

Twelve months passed. His hair turned white. He walked alone, his arms folded behind his back, jerking his head from side to side. One day he spoke to two other parish clients. He was bitter against his wife. She had gone out to wash for twelve shillings a week; the parish took back ten. 'She swears she'll shame me into doing something,' he said. 'She says I could easily slip out of town each weekend and play at some free-and-easy; earn a few bob that way.' His eyes blazed. 'The woman doesn't know what she's talking about. She's mad. Play a lot of maudlin rubbish to rowdy sots. And then go round with the hat. My God. I won't do it. I WON'T. NO.'

 He lowered his voice. 'Don't mind me too much, friend,' he said, 'only I must talk to someone.'

The pianist's mania was music. Beethoven was his favourite composer. He would suddenly halt in the middle of the footwalk, his eyes aglow. 'Do you know this tune?' he'd ask them. 'Tra-la-la-la, tra-la-la-la, la-la-Ia-la?' His hands would beat the air, his fingers jumping on an imaginary keyboard. 'A marvellous piece of work. Only a genius could write like that.'

The two men had never heard of Beethoven but they enjoyed such enthusiastic rendering. 'That's music,' he'd say, 'real music. And the damned fool people throw that over for hip-noise. Hip-noise, that's all it is; something to wag their backside to like bushmen jigging in the Congo. Oh God, I could SCREAM.' His fists would shoot up to his head.

His two companions realised that he must keep in practice. They sought out acquaintances with pianos and invited him to call round and comment on their tone. Opening the lid, he would strike the keys. If the tone was passable, he sat down on the stool and played into a world of his own. If one of the listeners spoke he would swing round, glaring, then bend his full weight over the keys. As he played his body straightened up, his fingers' touch grew lighter and, as he sat smiling absently to himself, the listeners nodded to each other with delight.

One night in a little parlour he found a piano that gave him joy. His fingers glided over the keys until he was one with his instrument. Six men sat listening intently; four of them were on the parish; the other two, sons of the house, had jobs.

The woman from the next house poked her frowsy head into the parlour. 'Oh,' she exclaimed, 'I didn't know there was company. Are you having a do? Can the quare feller play Swanee?'

The pianist swung round, his eyes flaming. 'Swanee!' he yelled. 'Bah,' he spat and swung back to the keyboard as if to bury himself in it, pounding the notes at lightning speed. His temper came through the music.

The frowsy woman, shocked, turned to one of the sons. 'Are you deaf, Tommy?' she shouted, 'letting him carry on like that. He wouldn't do it if yer mother was in. Where in God's name did yer pick 'im up?'

The pianist swung round on the stool. 'Get out,' he snarled. 'GET OUT.'

The woman clutched the tops of her blouse together. 'Well, I like that,' she said. 'Go away you bloody barm-pot, it's a hammer you should have. You want locking up.' She bounced out along the lobby, muttering to herself. The pianist shrugged his shoulders, then bent down to the music again.

A few weeks later he disappeared from the parish. The two men learned he had left town to play at the free and easys. Months afterwards, on the dock road, they spotted him. He was dragging a handcart piled with wire hawsers, his back bent low with straining to keep up with the horse lorries.

The men hailed him. He stopped, smiled feebly, and pulled over to the kerb. The sweat streamed from him. One of the men stared at the heavy hawsers. 'There's at least half a ton on there,' he said. 'What made you take on a job like this? Your hands will be murdered in no time.'

The pianist flared up. 'My hands?' he replied. 'My hands? Who the hell cares about my hands? No one. Not even me.' He quietened down. 'Oh, yes. You do. You two. But that's all. No one else.'

The flow of traffic forced him to struggle for a foothold. The men started him off with a push. As they walked alongside him, one of them jokingly remarked, 'Old Beethoven would hardly recognise you now.'

The pianist raised his face as if trying to remember something. Then a smile crossed his lips. 'Oh, yes,' he said, 'Beethoven. Ha, ha, ha, ha. Beethoven in a handcart. Damned good. Ha, ha, ha, ha, ha.' And he laughed and laughed until his face went blank again. The men bid him 'Ta-ra' and walked away, disheartened.

They lost trace of him for a year. Then one of them in a shopping street saw him crossing the tram-lines. His clothes were dirty and threadbare. His eyes, bulging and blood-streaked, seemed overbig in his bearded face. The other man hurriedly asked him how he was doing.

The pianist's eyes shone. Elbows pressed against his sides, his half-clenched fists jerked up and down in front of him.

'My hands are on the wheel that is steering the Universe,' he declared. 'One twist and I can destroy mankind, all these people passing by.'

The other man patted his shoulder. 'That wouldn't do you much good,' he said. 'You'd destroy yourself as well.'

The pianist's face set. 'You're wrong, my friend,' he declared. 'I am the indestructible. I am in control.'

A tram-driver clanged his bell. The pianist had to be led on to the pavement and left there, his hands still gripping an imaginary wheel that was keeping the Universe from disaster.

James Maury 1823

By the By: the warmth of our fireside in Rodney street prevented me from estimating fairly that of the mail coach, for I had not proceeded as far as Ben Bone's before I put on your comforter which you *forced* on me; it remained on my neck until I got to this house and I should have been very *uncomfortable* without it...

Dirk Pieter Van den Bergh 1906

We observed quickly that we were not staying in the neighborhood of a rich Heerengracht in Amsterdam. The glass of the windows of the stores were so dirty you could hardly see through them. We saw many butcher shops. They must consume an amazing amount of meat in Liverpool, because we saw an unusual number of them; but in all, one more unsanitary than the other. Where in Holland, the butcher shops have plate glass it is here just an open space. During the day that opening hangs full with carcasses of sheep and beef and partly outside and partly inside a wide shelf on which lay displayed different cuts of meat – weight marked with price tags. Meat seems fairly low-cost here; and so it lays there exposed to the sun and not less to the dust. Some pieces are already covered with dust and dirt.

Following this short inspection tour, we return back to our hotel or rather an abode, called hotel. It was time for our breakfast. The menu consisted of white bread, jam and coffee and was of good taste and quality. The complete absence of plates and unfresh looking table cover did not help to enjoy our food. After the breakfast was over, we went down town.

Our wives and the younger children stayed home. The sky was overcast and a thick haze was hanging in the streets, one could plainly see the smoke and inhale or breathe smoke. We could not see further than 150 to 200 feet into the rather wide streets. Naturally, our first plan was to go and see the Consul; his office was also filled with coal fumes.

Mr Kalis informed us that the Consul was not in and most likely would not come, with the damp and overcast sky. Since we had learned already in one situation, we realized he could not do any more for; we bid Mr Kalis farewell and returned to the street. We were in the center of the city. What a busy place and what a traffic! Thousands of freight wagons with big horses were pulling heavy freight wagons through the city. Some wagons were pulled by 2 and

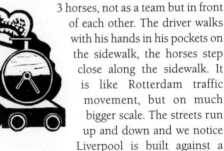

3 horses, not as a team but in front of each other. The driver walks with his hands in his pockets on the sidewalk, the horses step close along the sidewalk. It is like Rotterdam traffic movement, but on much bigger scale. The streets run up and down and we notice Liverpool is built against a mountain. All the streets are dirty; the horses sometimes slip and stumble. Hundreds of electric trams in noisy speed cross through the city which makes it very dangerous and unsafe for the big crowds of pedestrians. All trams are double deckers; we never see two trams connected together. Sometimes you see four or five street tram cars close behind

one another speeding along similar as you can see in Amsterdam on the Dam square. The bell, they use very little; each pedestrian has to look out for himself. All store display windows because of the damp smoke and dirt that hangs over the streets are covered with a dirty film. In the downtown and heart of the city are all stores, among which there were very nice ones, but in general does not compare with Amsterdam. If we could think of Liverpool and imagine it without fog and smoke it would really be an impressive city. Broad avenues and beautiful squares. Elegant architectural-designed monumental buildings and structures. But too bad, it all is covered by a film of soot and looks dirty.

Margi Clarke   1980s

The Thatcher experiment unpicked every stitch in the jumper of socialism but Liverpool resisted. We understand why the group has to be strong because the individual is only as strong as the group it comes from.

Barry Unsworth   1752

'The trade is wide open. Wide open, I tell you, gentlemen. The colonies grow more populous by the year, by the month. The more land that is planted, the more they will want negroes. It is a case of first come, first served. And who is best placed to take it on? London is away there on the wrong side, with the Thames up her arse. Bristol's costs are twice ours here. I tell you, if God picked this town up in the palm of his hand and studied where best in England to set her down for the Africa trade, he would put her exactly back where she is, exactly where she stands at present.'

Friedrich Engels   1844

In the other great seaport towns the prospect is no better. Liverpool, with all its commerce, wealth, and grandeur yet treats its workers with the same barbarity. A full fifth of the population, more than 45,000 human beings, live in narrow, dark, damp, badly-ventilated cellar dwellings, of which there are 7,862 in the city. Besides these cellar dwellings there are 2,270 courts, small spaces built up on all four sides and having but one entrance, a narrow, covered passage-way, the whole ordinarily very dirty and inhabited exclusively by proletarians.

John Cornelius   1981

We gaze through the top landing window, aghast. A sobering sense of seeing what must be history in the making vies for supremacy with a realistic, immediate desire to panic.

Outside, the entire skyline is an angry crimson. Dense, almost tangible, banks of black smoke hang threateningly above the rooftops. The silhouette of Tiber Street School, five hundred yards away, is framed by huge tongues of green and lilac flame, licking skyward. Over there by the Anglican Cathedral is a colossal blaze, the like of which we've never seen in our lives. By its position, we guess it must be the Rialto building going up. Almost as huge is the conflagration over in Parliament Street where there is a tyre factory and a couple of petrol stations... Lodge Lane is enveloped in dense smoke.

My adventure in the News-Room in the Exchange, which I have related in a previous chapter, reminds me of another, at the Lyceum, some days after, which may as well be put down here, before I forget it.

I was strolling down Bold-street, I think it was, when I was struck by the sight of a brown stone building, very large and handsome. The windows were open, and there, nicely seated, with their comfortable legs crossed over their comfortable knees, I beheld several sedate, happy-looking old gentlemen reading the magazines and papers, and one had a fine gilded volume in his hand.

Yes, this must be the Lyceum, thought I; let me see. So I whipped out my guide-book, and opened it at the proper plate; and sure enough, the building before me corresponded stone for stone. I stood awhile on the opposite side of the street, gazing at my picture, and then at its original; and often dwelling upon the pleasant gentlemen sitting at the open windows; till at last, I felt an uncontrollable impulse to step in for a moment, and run over the news.

'I'm a poor, friendless sailor-boy, thought I, and they can not object; especially as I am from a foreign land, and strangers ought to be treated with courtesy. I turned the matter over again, as I walked across the way; and with just a small tapping of a misgiving at my heart, I at last scraped my feet clean against the curb-stone, and taking off my hat while I was yet in the open air, slowly sauntered in.

But I had not got far into that large and lofty room, filled with many agreeable sights, when a crabbed old gentleman lifted up his eye from the *London Times*, which words I saw boldly printed on the back of the large sheet in his hand, and looking at me as if I were a strange dog with a muddy hide, that had stolen out of the gutter into this fine apartment, he shook his silver-headed cane at me fiercely, till the spectacles fell off his nose. Almost at the same moment, up stepped a terribly cross man, who looked as if he had a mustard plaster on his back, that was continually exasperating him; who throwing down some papers which he had been filing, took me by my innocent shoulders, and then, putting his foot against the broad part of my pantaloons, wheeled me right out into the street, and dropped me on the walk, without so much as offering an apology for the affront. I sprang after him, but in vain; the door was closed upon me.

These Englishmen have no manners, that's plain, thought I; and I trudged on down the street in a reverie.

David Sheppard   1975

In our first year in Liverpool, we went to see *Love and Kisses*

from Kirkby at the Everyman Theatre. We saw the first residents insisting that everyone take off their shoes before entering the sparkling new homes that were replacing their old terraced houses. And then we saw the disappointments follow – no repairs, no jobs – that spoiled the dream of a New Jerusalem.

John Newton 1755

I entered upon business yesterday. I find my duty is to attend the tides one week, and visit the ships that arrive, and such as are in the river; and the other week to inspect the vessels in the docks; and thus alternatively the year round. The latter is little more than a sinecure, but the former requires pretty constant attendance, both by day and night. I have a good office, with fire and candle, fifty or sixty people under my direction, with a handsome six-oared boat and a coxswain to row me about in form. Mr. W. went with me on my first cruise down to the Rock. We saw a vessel, and wandered upon the hills till she came in. I then went on board, and performed my office with all due gravity; and had it not been my business, the whole might have passed for a party of pleasure.

Tracey Emin 2006

I've been in Liverpool judging the John Moores painting competition. My fellow judges were (and will be again) Sir Peter Blake, or the great Papa Smurf of Pop Art, as we like to call him, Andrea Rose from the British Council and the painter Jason Brookes. We spent three days, from early morning to late evening, in a dark room, looking at more than

3,000 slides. This column is very difficult for me to write at the moment as I keep finding myself nodding and saying: 'Yes. No. Yes – yes – no.' And last night in Liverpool, in a Chinese restaurant, I realised that myself and my fellow judges were transfixed by a glass door with fish on it. And after a short pause, in complete unison, we all nodded and said: 'Yes.'

Julius Rodenberg 1856

As we returned home through the illuminated alleys along the shore, music sounded – especially the shrill bagpipe – from the taverns where the sailors were drinking, singing and dancing. In Liverpool, all my real joy came only from the sea, but in order not to seem more impolite than I was, I still had to express joy or wonder at many things which the Liverpudlians have to show to their guests. Nowhere can one get a better picture of the incessant bustle of a port than here. One street is inhabited entirely by negroes and half-castes, three or four others by perpetually drunken prostitutes, a whole district consists of shop after shop, supplying the departing seaman and his ship for the journey round the world, or providing long-missed delights for the home-comer. Out of this tangle of mostly narrow and dirty alleys rise two imposing buildings, the Custom House – a toll-house I believe even more important than the one in London – and the Sailor's Home, a barracks-like institution established by Prince Albert, in which sailors can find accommodation safe against theft and other accidents for the duration of their stay ashore.

Rachel Kempson 1935

From Gambia Terrace you could see beyond the bulky, red cathedral then half built, down to the Mersey River. The stone birds on the Liver Building near the quay gleamed white in the sun. As it was such a lovely morning I decided to walk down the hill to the Playhouse instead of taking a tram, so I set off along the terrace, turning left into the main street which went straight into the city. It had rained during the night, and so the air was clear and the streets looked washed. There were streets and streets of shabby-looking Georgian houses. Their windows were beautifully proportioned and many doors had fine fanlights, but the buildings were all covered with the black smoke and grime given off by the factory chimneys in all northern towns. Even in the most prosperous streets the houses looked grim and forbidding. However, as I walked down the hill in the sun I felt far from depressed. I was full of that nervous excitement that precedes any new venture in the theatre.

We started for Liverpool. Its name denotes an old pond, and, in truth, the flat damp country, bathed in sea-mist and covered with stagnant water, seems less adapted for men than for wild-duck. Now and then the land appears primeval; untilled downs and sandy-bogs are to be seen; the region, unenclosed, terminates at the horizon in a faint streak of pale verdure. Heavy violet-tinted clouds, exhalations of the sea and the soil, as in Holland, fill and dim the space which stretches beneath the low canopy of sky and the limitless plain.

At the entrance to the city there is a huge Grecian building, a sort of temple with gilt panels, and pillars in imitation jasper, and serving as a concert-hall. In it a frightfully harsh-toned organ makes a din. On the opposite side, in front, is a library which cost £50,000, the legacy of a private individual. This is not the place to seek beauty and elegance. Liverpool is a giant, like Manchester; the shops and warehouses are on a vast scale; the streets are vast, and the houses which line them resemble those of London in being overladen with arcades, pillars, and pilasters, the effect produced on the beholder being an impression of crowding and heaviness. The inhabitants number 500,000, and the port is the most frequented after that of London.

Along the docks the cotton warehouses form a kind of

cyclopian, endless and monotonous rampart; nearly all the cotton of the world is housed here. But the appearance of the docks themselves effaces everything. The Mersey, as large as an arm of the sea, stretches towards the west, carrying vessels away and bearing them home. For a distance of six miles along its bank these vessels pass through canals into basins lined with stone, resembling watery streets and squares, multiplied and ramified, wherein they are repaired or discharge their cargoes. Their closely-packed masts appear like a forest in winter, extending as far as the eye can reach, and blocking up the entire horizon towards the north. Yet the spacious and numerous docks do not suffice to contain the multitude of ships; they are crowded together in rows and masses at the entrances, awaiting their turn to pass in; at Birkenhead, on the opposite bank, new docks are being built for their accommodation.

I believe this spectacle to be one of the grandest in the world. Some of the vessels are 3,500, others 4,000 tons burden. A steamer is upwards of 300 feet in length. A vessel at anchor, the *Great Britain*, is about to carry 1,200 emigrants to Australia. If one descends the dry docks to the keels of the ships, one perceives that the hull is from forty to fifty feet in height. The swelling and copper-sheathed sides have the fine curves of a sea-bird about to slumber upon the waves.

The view from Birkenhead commands the harbour, and the vast reach of the river; it is rather agitated, and gleams with yellow lustre, amid a slight haze. The steamboats ascend and descend, cross and re-cross, with stiff mechanical movements, like black crabs. Sailing ships, lightly heeling over, skim along like beautiful swans. The *George*, a man-of-war carrying 86 guns, arrives in lordly style, all the others making way for her. On the other side the boundless row of masts and rigging lines the sky, while the huge city is massed behind.

We visit several workshops, among others, the establishment of Messrs. Laird, the builders of iron ships. It is said that within the last thirty years they have built two hundred and fifty; they employ fifteen hundred workpeople, have gigantic furnaces and machines, and have stocks, to which water is brought through canals. At present the hull of a paddle steamer is on the stocks, its length is 350 feet, and it is designed to make the passage between England and Ireland at the speed of twenty miles an hour. It will cost from £80,000 to £100,000, will be completed in six months; the iron compartments which contain the eight boilers are composed of metal beams as large as a man's body.

The same impression is always produced, that of hugeness. Yet do labour and power suffice to render a man happy? M.B––, a leading merchant, sits for three hours after dinner with his guests drinking port wine in silence. Another, whenever he can get away, rushes off to his country seat to brace up his nerves; he is enthusiastic about breeding pigs. When man is dissatisfied with his lot he seeks for compensation in dream-land. I was shown a spot where four or five preachers – Methodists for the most part – come to address a crowd on Sunday in the open air; the idea of the Kingdom of God, of the loving Christ, of the all-powerful and tender friend, is one refuge for distressed minds.

Another refuge is intoxication. The authoress of a 'Life for a Life' writes:- 'This Liverpool is an awful town for drinking. Other towns may be as bad; statistics prove it; but I know no place where intoxication is so open and shameless. Not only in bye streets and foul courts, where one expects to see it, but everywhere. I never take a short railway journey in the after part of the day but I am liable to meet at least one drunken 'gentleman' snoozing in his first-class carriage; or, in the second class, two or three drunken 'men', singing, swearing, or pushed stupidly about by pale-faced wives. The sadness of the thing is that the wives do not seem to mind it, that everybody takes it quite as a matter of course. The 'gentleman', often grey-haired, is but 'merry', as he is accustomed to be every night of his life; the poor man has only 'had a drop or two', as all his comrades are in the habit of taking whenever they get the chance; they see no disgrace in it, so they laugh at him a bit, and humour him, and are quite ready to stand up for him against all incomers who may object to such a fellow-passenger. *They* don't; nor do the women belonging to them, who are well-used to tolerate drunken sweethearts, and lead about and pacify drunken husbands.'

It is now six o'clock, and we return through the poorer quarter. What a sight! In the vicinity of Leeds Street there are fifteen or twenty streets across which cords are stretched and covered with rags and linen, hung up to dry. Bands of children swarm on every flight of steps, five or six are clustered on each step, the eldest holding the smallest; their faces are pale, their light hair in disorder, their clohes are in tatters, they have neither shoes nor stockings, and they are all shockingly dirty; their faces and hands appearing to be encrusted with dust and soot. Perhaps two hundred children romp and wallow in a single street. On nearer approach one sees one of the mothers and a grown-up sister, with little more covering than their chemises, crouching in the dusky passage. What interiors! They contain a little piece of worn oil-cloth, sometimes a shell ornament, one or two plaster ornaments; in the one corner is seated the idiot grandmother; the wife is busied in mending the wretched rags of clothing, the children push each other about. The smell resembles that of an old rag-shop. The ground-floor of nearly every dwelling is a flagged and damp basement. Can one imagine what life in these cellars must be during winter? Some of the younger children are still fresh and rosy, but their large blue eyes are painful to behold; their good blood will deteriorate; as they grow older they will waste away, the flesh becoming flabby and of an unhealthy pallor; many of their faces are scrofulous, being marked with small sores covered with plaister. As we proceed the crowd is more dense. Tall youths seated or half-crouching at the side of the pavement play with black cards. Old, bearded hags come out of the gin-shops; their legs totter; their dull looks and besotted smile are indescribable: it appears as if their features had been slowly eaten away by vitriol. The rags which they wear are falling to pieces, displaying their filthy skins; these were once the fashionable dresses of fine ladies. A shocking detail is that these streets are built with regularity, and have a modern aspect; probably this is a quarter modernised and rendered more airy by a beneficent municipality; such, then, is the best that can be done for the poor. The uniform row of buildings and pavements borders the two sides of the way, inclosing in its mathematical lines this teeming heap of horrors and human wretchedness. The air is close and oppressive, the light wan and dim; there is not a tint or a shape on which the eye can rest with pleasure; Rembrandt's beggars were far better off in their picturesque holes.

Margaret Thatcher 1981

My right honourable friend the Home Secretary fully endorsed the action of the use of CS gas on Merseyside. We are now considering what other equipment the police may need. The use of water cannon is certainly not ruled out.

Oliver Lodge c1883

I sometimes lectured five hours a day; even the standing up all that time was tiring. I had to walk the two or three miles from home to college, lunch as best I could, and then walk home again in the evening – sometimes, I remember, being very tired. There were no trams in those days, nor any means of conveyance except an occasional, rather expensive cab. The walk was not unpleasant, however, as it led through Prince's Avenue, along one side of Prince's Park, and so through a corner of Sefton Park, or else Ullet Road, along Linnet Lane to Lark Lane, and the Waverley district, where the streets were named after Walter Scott's novels – Bertram Road,

Mannering Road, Ivanhoe Road, and others. The so-called lanes were also named systematically after birds, Ullet being probably a contraction of owlet. Sefton Park was a joy to the children, many of whose memories must be associated with that place. And even I on Sundays remember the walks through lilac and laburnum in full bloom. It had not been opened very long, and was a wonderful lung to the city, admirably laid out with grottos and a lake and a stream running through it. It was spacious enough for a novice to be able to lose himself. Along many of the roads through the park, horse-traffic was forbidden, so that the place was safe for children.

Kenny Everett   c1960

I used to think caftans were the thing to wear, all loose and flowy and easy to put on. But, of course, I'd have been lynched for wearing anything like that in Liverpool. That's another daft thing: nobody objected to people walking around in shoes which piled your toes on top of one another, and with mounds of white margarine in your hair, but if you'd trolled down Lime Street in a caftan – WALLOP!

Johanna Schopenhauer   1803

The topics of conversation in Liverpool are perhaps slightly lighter than London. Here, as there, however, the discussion usually drifts towards issues common to all, so that the foreigner can swiftly join in the conversation. Once the usual topic of conversation (which in this country is dictated by etiquette, such as weather and good health) has been discussed, you

would find yourself in a very regrettable position if you had no knowledge of, or interest in, trade and politics.

Almost all the men of this city have travelled and seen foreign countries, know about foreign custom and traditions, which makes them more tolerant towards foreigners. The women on the other hand are truly English in the full meaning of the word, and they lack higher education which is easier to access in big cities such as London than in provincial ones. To make up for it, they have created for themselves thousands of needs and affectations to express both their wealth and good position in society, but that would make someone unaware of those manners feel uncomfortable and embarrassed.

The virtue of freedom is highly valued by the Liverpudlians which other Englishmen don't have nor aim at obtaining. However, it can't be denied that boredom presides here until the dinner table is vacated by the ladies, leaving elbow-room for the gentlemen to drink wine and discuss politics.

George Orwell   1936

I was impressed by the fact that Liverpool is doing much more in the way of slum-clearance than most towns. The slums are still very bad but there are great quantities of Corporation houses and flats at low rents. Just outside Liverpool there are quite considerable towns consisting entirely of Corporation houses, which are really quite livable and decent to look at, but having as usual the objection that they take people a long way from their work. In the centre of the town there are huge blocks of workers' flats imitated from those in Vienna. They are built in the form of an immense ring, five storeys high, round a central courtyard about 60 yards across, which forms a playground for children. Round the inner side run balconies, and there are wide windows on each side so that everyone gets some sunlight.

Jean-Michel Dutens   1819

In the reign of Queen Anne, Liverpool constructed a dock to shelter storm-tossed vessels: she now has eight of them, and will soon have thirteen, not counting the extensions of the older ones, which will have a total area of 200,000 square metres.

The works which are now going on for the dock called the Regent's Dock, which is to be 500 yards long by 110 yards wide, are being carried out with great skill by Mr. Foster. One finds in the way they are managed that same progress in the art whose benefits I remarked upon at the ports of Chatham and Plymouth. They are spending 200,000 francs a month on the work at Liverpool.

The materials used in the works are of the finest quality. The freestone, a dense and very homogeneous sandstone, comes from quarries on the opposite coast, only one and a half leagues away. In their foundation work they make extensive use of a mortar invented by Messrs Parker and Wyat, of London, known in England as Roman Cement. This cement is made up of one part volcanic rock from the Isle of Sheppey, two leagues from Sheerness, which is burned and ground like limestone; one part limestone and two parts of sand. The proportions are varied according to the nature of the work.

The workmen are served by a system of railways, some built on the level and some on inclined planes. Mr. Foster Jnr. told me that their total length was no less than three miles. These railways are made like all the others, with a bar 14 centimetres wide and an upstand or raised edge to restrain the wagons, and about a metre long. These bars are layed on transverse timbers. They cost, including those parts requiring points or turntables, ten shillings per yard run, or 13.52 francs per metre. That amounts to a total of 65,261.04 francs, which is not a great expense when one takes into account that the components of these railways will last more or less forever, and besides, they suffer only a very slight diminution in their weight and hence their value.

Sitting in a soft-stripped flat on the 21st floor of a semi-abandoned tower block in the Kensington district of Liverpool I am temporarily the highest resident on Merseyside. I can see the sunlight dapple the flanks of Snowdon nigh on 70 miles to the south. I can see the Wirral like a spatulate tongue licking the Irish Sea. I can see the Mersey itself, coursing through its trough of defunct docks. Towards Bootle the gargantuan sails of wind turbines look like propellers powering the upside down burgh through the steely grey sky. Ranged across the mid-ground are the signature buildings of the city: the Liver Buildings with their sentinel herons; the mucoid concrete of the hospital; the dirty white stalk of the radio station with its restaurant revolving like a conjurer's plate; and the two cathedrals, one the outhouse of the morally relativist gods, the other a split yoghurt pot oozing spiritual culture.

The graticule of streets spreads out from the base of my tower, a tight stacking of tiled roofs which gleam wet with rain. I sit here from dawn to dusk watching the weather systems roll in, completely divorced from the human life of the city. The block will soon be demolished. Twenty years ago tens of these concrete snaggle teeth gnashed Liverpool's flesh – but they've mostly been extracted. Draughts sough in the empty corridors and cavernous stairwells. As the block is emptied out – so is the city itself; and despite endless talk of regeneration, the fact remains that Liverpool has halved in population since the Second World War. To apprehend this you have only to observe the slow trickle of outward-bound traffic which is the rush hour, or descend into the financial district at 5.30pm, where you'll find hardly anyone at all. The impressive Victorian municipal buildings lower in the dusk, stage sets for an epic long since wrapped.

Occasionally the Wirral is too tantalising and I grab my foldaway bicycle, sprint to the lift, plummet to the ground, freewheel all the way down the hill to the Pier Head and take the ferry across the Mersey. 'Ferry, 'cross the Mersey!' sings Gerry over the Tannoy, while the Pacemakers plink-plonk their accompaniment. This is a moment of maximum urban quiddity, the song hymning the vehicle while you're actually

on it. It's like a busker singing 'Streets of London' in the streets of London, at once sweetly homely and infinitely claustrophobic. But all too soon we've heaved to at Seacombe and I'm pedalling along the magnificently sculpted

Wallasey Embankment past the tidy villas of Egremont. On and on, the peninsula curving and curving to my left as I circumvent the last resort of New Brighton.

Empty sky, flat sea, sharp wind. The occasional lonely walker head bowed to escape the oppression of the sky. If I felt alone in the echoing precincts of the city, I now feel completely abandoned. On the outskirts of Hoylake a fat middle manager sleeps off his expense-account pub lunch slumped in his Vauxhall Omega, while I take a piss in a WC acrid with fresh saltwater and ancient urine. I thought I might walk from the point across to the tidal island of Hilbre, there to commune with seals, but in the event my timing is wrong, so I cycle to the station, fold the bike up and take the train back into the centre.

At Birkenhead we descend clanking into the tunnel under the Mersey, and suddenly all is echoing expanses of white tiling, festoons of cabling, and glimpses of tortuous machinery which suggest the dystopic vision of Piranesi. Intended for a far larger population the superb local rail system of Merseyside is housed in caverns beneath the city itself, a ghost train endlessly circumnavigating the interior of this dark star of urbanity. But as if these tunnels, and the Queensway road tunnel under the river, weren't enough of a vermiculation, in the last few years a group of enthusiastic volunteers have been opening up the Williamson Tunnels. These brick-lined conduits were built by a local magnate during the early decades of the 19th century. Some say they were a labour-creating project, a piece of proto-Keynesianism, intended to provide employment for soldiers returned from the Napoleonic wars. Others aver that Williamson himself was a Millenarian, and that the tunnels were intended as a refuge for Liverpudlians from the coming apocalypse.

If the Tunnels' genesis is in dispute, then so is their extent. Some claim there's only a few hundred metres of them, but others swear that the whole fabric of the city is riddled like a vast Emmental cheese. Whatever the truth of the matter, the Tunnels are a curious complement to the depopulation of Liverpool, an introjection of the municipality's own sense of its emptiness; after all, if so many people have vanished, where can they possibly have gone to?

Dr William Henry Duncan 1842

From the absence of drains and sewers, there are of course few cellars entirely free from damp; many of those in low situations are literally inundated after a fall of rain. To remedy the evil, the inhabitants frequently make little holes or wells at the foot of the cellar steps or in the floor itself; and notwith-standing these contrivances, it has been necessary in some cases to take the door off its hinges and lay it on the floor supported by bricks, in order to protect the inhabitants from the wet. Nor is this the full extent of the evil; the fluid matter of the court privies sometimes oozes through into the adjoin-ing cellars, rendering them uninhabitable by any one whose olfactories retain the slightest sensibility. In one cellar in Lace-street I was told that the filthy water thus collected measured not less than two feet in depth; and in another cellar, a well, four feet deep, into which this stinking fluid was allowed to drain, was discovered below the bed where the family slept!

George Melly c1932

Surrounded by large late nineteenth-century houses, ringed by a sandy ride where middle-class little girls cantered self-consciously past on horses hired from a local riding school, Sefton Park forms a valley bisected by a string of lakes, the largest of which, 'The Big Lake', had boats for hire in summer and, when frozen in the winter, became black with skaters. On the other side of the lakes, dominating the landscape, is the Palm House, a large, circular, domed building of steel and glass in imitation of the Crystal Palace. When it was cold it offered a steamy refuge to expressionless men in bright blue

suits and red ties, many of them missing an arm or leg. They were the institutionalised wounded of the 1914-18 war, and would sit all day smoking Woodbines on the fern-patterned Victorian benches. Behind them grew a contained circular jungle, its tropical trees and plants neatly labelled, and here and there a small marble statue of a coy nymph or simpering maiden with a quotation from a poet carved on her plinth. In summer the men sat outside on similar benches.

Statues ringed the exterior also, life-size and representing historic figures in the arts and sciences. Before I could read, my father invented false identities for those frozen worthies. A Swiss botanist, he assured me, represented the Prince of Wales, while Galileo, holding a globe of the world, he maintained to be Dixie Dean, the celebrated footballer. Beyond the Palm House the park levelled out to form a great plain big enough to accommodate the annual fair; below it a steep hill swept down to one of the little lakes.

At the bottom of this hill were two stone posts designed to discourage cyclists as there was then only a few yards across a road before the iron railings which ringed the water. I had at one time a small yellow motor car with push pedals and on one of our visits to look at Dixie Dean and the Prince of Wales my father made the following proposition. He would squat behind me on the yellow pedal car, in itself a rather precarious operation, and we would then free-wheel down the hill between the posts, whereupon I would have to turn the wheel abruptly to the right in order to avoid the railings. At five or six, for I can't have been any older, this seemed a perfectly reasonable if exciting thing to do, for I trusted Tom entirely and the danger didn't occur to me. We did it, gathering considerable speed, and shot between the posts missing the railings by a few inches. The mystery is that I cannot imagine what got into my father. It was most unlike him, and either or both of us could have been killed or badly injured. He told me not to tell my mother who wouldn't understand and I never did. Perhaps though, like Maud's driving, it is a false memory.

Most visits to the park were less traumatic. Accompanied by my mother or a nanny we usually carried with us one of those creased and crinkly brown paper bags (no longer manufactured) full of crusts cut from sandwiches, and any stale bread on the point of claiming Mrs Spilsbury's attention. This was to feed the ducks, and was indeed known as 'the ducks' bread', but very little of it reached the throng of mallards, Canadian geese and the odd swan for whom it was intended. En route, almost before we had reached the bottom of Lark Lane, my brother and I and later my sister had eaten most of it. We wouldn't have looked at it in the ordinary way, of course, but in the open air (and because it was for the

ducks) it tasted delicious. The phrase 'the ducks' bread'
became in time shorthand for any eating up of stale or
rejected food. My mother had a loathing of waste and would
finish anything left on a plate or about to be thrown away.
Such odds and ends – a spoonful of steak and kidney pie,
some congealed custard, a wilting salad – never reached the
dustbin. 'Your mother,' Tom would say on catching her
guiltily but obsessively spooning them up, 'is at the ducks'
bread again.'

The Park, like much of Liverpool, paid its reluctant
homage to London. The sandy perimeter ride was called
'Rotten Row'. At the end of the 'little lakes' was a cast of
Kensington Garden's Peter Pan. During my childhood, a full-
sized replica of Piccadilly's Eros was installed opposite the
café at the bottom of the hill which led down from the Lark
Lane gates. The café was rebuilt at the same time. The
wooden 'Elizabethan' shack was replaced by a more solid
art-deco structure. Peter Pan and Eros belong for me in
Sefton Park. When later I saw the originals *in situ* I thought
of them as 'displaced'.

Charles Dickens 1860

It was a Friday night, and Friday night was considered not a
good night for Jack. At any rate, Jack did not show in very
great force even here, though the house was one to which he
much resorts, and where a good deal of money is taken.
There was British Jack, a little maudlin and sleepy, lolling over
his empty glass, as if he were trying to read his fortune at the
bottom; there was Loafing Jack of the Stars and Stripes, rather
an unpromising customer, with his long nose, lank cheek,

high cheek-bones, and nothing soft about him but his cabbage-leaf hat; there was Spanish Jack, with curls of black hair, rings in his ears, and a knife not far from his hand, if you get into trouble with him; there were Maltese Jack, and Jack of Sweden, and Jack the Finn, looming through the smoke of their pipes, and turning faces that looked as if they were carved out of dark wood, towards the young lady dancing the hornpipe: who found the platform so exceedingly small for it, that I had a nervous expectation of seeing her, in the backward steps, disappear through the window. Still, if all hands had been got together, they would not have more than half-filled the room. Observe, however, said Mr. Licensed Victualler, the host, that it was Friday night, and, besides, it was getting on for twelve, and Jack had gone aboard. A sharp and watchful man, Mr. Licensed Victualler, the host, with tight lips and a complete edition of Cocker's arithmetic in each eye. Attended to his business himself, he said. Always on the spot. When he heard of talent, trusted nobody's account of it but went off by rail to see it. If true talent, engaged it. Pounds a week for talent – four pound – five pound. Banjo Bones was undoubted talent. Hear this instrument that was going to play – it was real talent! In truth it was very good; a kind of piano-accordion, played by a young girl of a delicate prettiness of face,  figure, and dress, that made the audience look coarser. She sang to the instrument, too; first, a song about village bells, and how they chimed; then a song about how I went to sea; winding up with an imitation of the bagpipes, which Mercantile Jack seemed to understand much the best. A good girl, said Mr. Licensed Victualler. Kept herself select. Sat in Snug, not listening to the blandishments of Mates. Lived with mother. Father dead. Once a merchant well to do, but over-speculated himself. On delicate inquiry as to salary paid for item of talent under consideration, Mr. Victualler's pounds dropped suddenly to shillings – still it was a very comfort-able thing for a young person like that, you know; she only went on six times a night, and was only required to be there from six at night to twelve. What was more conclusive was, Mr. Victualler's assurance that he 'never allowed any language, and never suffered any disturbance.' Sharpeye confirmed the statement, and the order that prevailed was the best proof of it that could have been cited. So, I came to the conclusion that poor Mercantile Jack might do (as I am afraid he does) much worse than trust himself to Mr. Victualler, and pass his evenings here.

Beryl Bainbridge   1944

They went down hill towards the river. Passing the old black houses built by the shipping owners, four-storeys high with pillars at the front door and steps of granite – occupied now by riff-raff: washing hung sodden on the wrought-iron balconies, a pram with three wheels in the gutter, a running herd of children without shoes. Some of the railings had been taken away to be melted down for the war-effort and there was wire meshing to stop people breaking their necks in the blackout. There was the new Cathedral rising like an ocean liner out of the sunken graveyard, tethered to its dry dock by giant cranes, coloured all over a soft and rusty pink.

Josephine Butler 1866

I went down to the oakum sheds and begged admission. I was taken into an immense gloomy vault filled with women and girls – more than two hundred probably at that time. I sat on the floor among them and picked oakum. They laughed at me, and told me my fingers were of no use for that work, which was true. But while we laughed we became friends. I proposed that they should learn a few verses to say to me on my next visit. I recollect a tall, dark, handsome girl standing up in our midst, among the damp refuse and lumps of tarred rope, and repeating without a mistake and in a not unmusical voice, clear and ringing, that wonder-ful fourteenth chapter of St. John's Gospel – the words of Jesus – all through, ending with. 'Peace I leave with you. My peace I give unto you. Let not your heart be troubled, neither let it be afraid...' She had selected it herself, and they listened in perfect silence, this audience – wretched, draggled, ignorant, criminal, some wild, and defiant others. The tall, dark-haired girl had prepared the way for me, and I said, 'now let us all kneel and cry to the same Jesus who spoke those words'; and down on their knees they fell, every one of them, reverently, on that damp stone floor, some saying the words after me, others moaning and weeping. It was a strange sound, that united wail – continuous, pitiful, strong – like a great sigh or murmur of vague desire and hope, issuing from the heart of despair, piercing the gloom and murky atmosphere of that vaulted room, and reaching to the heart of God.

Thomas Creevey 1822

We all dined at Knowsley last night. The new dining-room is opened: it is 53 feet by 37, and such a height that it destroys the effect of all the other apartments... You enter it from a passage by two great Gothic church-like doors the whole height of the room. This entrance is in itself fatal to the effect. Ly. Derby (like herself), when I objected to the immensity of the doors, said: 'You've heard Genl. Grosvenor's remark upon them, have you not? He asked in his grave, pompous manner – "Pray are those great doors to be opened for every pat of butter that comes into the room?"'

Ralph Waldo Emerson 1856

I remarked the stoutness, on my first landing at Liverpool; porter, drayman, coachman, guard, – what substantial, respectable, grandfatherly figures, with costume and manners to suit. The American has arrived at the old mansion-house, and finds himself among uncles, aunts, and grandsires. The pictures on the chimney-tiles of his nursery were pictures of these people. Here they are in the identical costumes and air which so took him.

Robert Carr Bosanquet 1918

What a gloomy anachronistic business this examining is! Here am I invigilating on a grey winter-like morning, sitting where the stage should be; and on the tiers of seats are young women in summer blouses, scribbling hard; whereas it would be much more appropriate if I sat up there and they performed a choric dance down here in the orchestra. Not all women – there are some men in khaki who have come back expressly; it must seem odd and unreal to them. This is my only morning of invigilating, and I shall be able to go this afternoon and hear Sir Randolf Baker, at the Town Hall, on the entertaining of the American troops. Did I tell thee I saw a contingent of Sammies march up on Tuesday evening, magnificent men just landed from the *Mauretania*, which was lying at the Pier Head, looking nearly as big as the Liver Building.

My neighbour at dinner last night was a Major Wrigley, keen naturalist, who has lived a long time at Freshfield, and told me a good deal about the birds and flowers. These links are a great place for flowers. One thing which I had found and asked about, grows only in one other place in the British

Isles, – a delicate stem with tiny pinkish-white bells, like an attenuated Lily of the Valley. There's a tern-ery, where the young are now newly hatched, which I must visit. Larks abound, plovers, shell-ducks, sand-pipers, owls, and all manner; but the characteristic bird of the golf-links is the cuckoo, which is heard night and day; and seen, especially in the evening. Several times when I've been out late I've seen one perched on a wooden shelter, uttering his note of despair, for I really think that's what it is. It's Mr Cuckoo who does all the ordinary calling; Mrs Cuckoo's note is much lower; and Mr Cuckoo says 'A woman's sphere is the home; what has become of my children?'

Asparagus appears every night at dinner, since we live in its native home. It has even run wild on the links, and someone suggested that, like seakale, it may originally have been a seaside plant.

Ann Maury 1832

March 1st. I thought much of home, recollecting the procession of Welshmen decorated with Onions who would on that day parade the streets of Liverpool in honour of their patron, St. David.

Nikolaus Pevsner 1969

Some are distinguished, some acceptable, some objectionable, but as a whole the university suffers from a nimiety of architects. The whole is not a whole but a zoo, with species after species represented. If only such a client trusted one architect more!

John James Audubon

Why should my feelings be so dampened tonight? Why, because it rains, and I have just reached the Commercial with a wet coat, wet waistcoat, shirt and skin. Had it not been for this natural incident in a country where I was told I never would see the sun shine, not a portion of my *tout ensemble* would have been in the least moist.

However, this rain was not a deluge such as we often experience in our warmer latitude. It does not stop a man from walking on. Quite to the contrary, it invites one to walk faster, unless he is provided with a sixteen shilling umbrella, in his hand and open, when he may take it leisurely – not like me and mine. Tonight my umbrella was dozing silently in the corner of my room, close by the washing stand. I walked fast, believe me!

The morning was beautiful, clear, pleasant. I was on the mound betimes, and saw the city plainly and the country beyond the Mersey quite plain also. When first I left the Inn the watchmen watched me, and perhaps thought that I was an owl caught out by the day, as I moved not like a meteor but like a man either in a hurry, or a flurry, or crazy. The fact is that I thought of nothing but the exhibition. Nothing else could have entered my brains.

The wind mills are very different here from the few I have seen in America, and so are the watchmen. Both, I think, are taller and fuller about the waist. I do not like four square angles breaking on the foreground of a landscape, and yet I was forced twice today to submit to that mortification. But to counterpoise this, I had the satisfaction of setting on the grass, to watch four truant boys rolling marbles with great spirit for a good full half hour. How they laughed, how briskly they moved, how much they brought from afar again my younger days. I would have liked them better still, at this innocent avocation, had they been decently clean, but they were not so, and I arose after giving them enough to purchase a shilling's worth of marbles.

Siegfried Sassoon 1916

The third winter of the war had settled down on the lines of huts with calamitous drabness; fog-bleared sunsets were succeeded by cavernous and dispiriting nights when there was nothing to do and nowhere to do it.

Crouching as close as I could to the smoky stove in my hut I heard the wind moaning around the roof, feet clumping cheerlessly along the boards of the passage, and all the systematized noises and clatterings and bugle-blowings of the Camp. Factory-hooters and ships' fog-horns out on the Mersey sometimes combined in huge  unhappy dissonances; their sound seemed one with the smoke-drifted munition-works, the rubble of industrial suburbs, and the canal that crawled squalidly out into blighted and forbidding farmlands which were only waiting to be built over.

Oliver Wendell Holmes   1886

When Dickens landed in Boston, he was struck with the brightness of all the objects he saw, – buildings, signs, and so forth. When I landed in Liverpool, everything looked very dark, very dingy, very massive, in the streets I drove through.

Private Eye   2004

'Boris Johnson shouldn't apologise to Liverpool for the *Spectator* leader,' Euan Ferguson wrote in the *Observer* on 17 October. 'He should apologise for remaining a member of a political party which deliberately tore the heart from that city and made it the vulnerable self it is today.'

But if everyone who offends Liverpool had to go on a penitential pilgrimage, half of Fleet Street would be on the next train to Lime Street. Including, er, Euan Ferguson – who on 20 October 2002 wrote this attack on John Lennon: 'It could be argued that it was his narcissistic emoting, never shot through with the tiniest ray of intellectual rigour, which began the Liverpudlianisation of Britain and turned us into a country that fills its gutters with tears for girls we've never met.'

That resonant coinage 'Liverpudlianisation' had first appeared, again in the *Observer*, on 5 October 1997 when Jonathan Meades argued that Tony Blair's religiosity 'accords perfectly with the Liverpudlianisation of Britain... no-holds-barred self-pity dressed as grief, self-congratulatory sentimentalism, an affirmation of itself through the appropri-ation of cosmetic Celtism'.

The *Observer*'s sister paper, the *Guardian*, has given Boris

Johnson a thorough kicking over the past fortnight. It condemned the *Spectator* editorial as 'insulting' and 'vile'. It also dispatched Ed Vulliamy to write a piece about how great Liverpool and Liverpudlians are. But amid all its sanctimonious tut-tutting over Boris's idiocy, there was no mention of the Grauniad's own articles on Liverpool, such as this from 24 May 1993: 'The royal family has taken its whacks with a certain decent cheerfulness, something which compares interestingly with the intimidatory self-pity issuing from Liverpool if anyone suggests that idle, violent city is, well, an idle, violent city and not a citadel of delightful Scouser wit and defiance.'

All a long time ago, of course. But surely the Grauniad can't have forgotten the column it published by Charlotte Raven on 26 June 2001? 'Scousers' propensity to linger over every misfortune until another comes to replace it makes them uniquely suited to the demands of the Bulger mourning marathon,' she wrote. 'While other cities might have faltered and found something else to distract them, Liverpool's talent for nursing resentments ensured that it would feel, eight years on, just as enraged about Bulger's murder as it was the first

moment it heard.' Liverpudlians, she added, refuse to let anything go 'as long as there's still a drop of righteous indignation to be squeezed'.

A few days later, after a deluge of protest, the readers' editor announced that Raven's piece should never have been printed. Yet, oddly enough, it can still be found on the paper's website. Perhaps the Grauniad assumes that Scousers are too poor or thick to have the internet.

Another newspaper which has shown Boris Johnson no mercy is the *Times*. Andrew Pierce warned that the *Spectator*'s 'ill-judged attack on Liverpool' had caused 'grievous offence', while Michael Gove denounced it as 'a misjudgment of quite stonking proportions'. Clearly the *Times* would never do anything so rash as to generalise about Scousers. Except that on 23 April 1989, after the Hillsborough disaster, it printed a column by Edward Pearce arguing that 'the shrine in the Anfield goalmouth, the cursing of the police, all the theatricals, come sweetly to a city which is already the world capital of self-pity. There are soapy politicians to make a pet of Liverpool, and Liverpool itself is always standing by to make a pet of itself. "Why us? Why are we treated like animals?" To which the plain answer is that a good and sufficient minority of you behave like animals.'

Four years later, Walter Ellis covered the Bulger murder for the *Times*. 'Liverpool lives on emotion; fears and hatreds bubble constantly below the surface,' he reported on 19 February 1993. 'The mob, as self-pitying as it is self-righteous, is a constant presence, whether on tour in the Heysel Stadium, Brussels, or at home among the social dereliction of Liverpool 8, or as this week in the back streets of Bootle.'

A 2,000-word *Times* feature by Michael Henderson on 21 November 1998 described Liverpool as 'a city that often gives the impression of wearing its decline as a badge of honour'. Henderson also quoted Alan Bennett, who had written of Liverpudlians' 'built-in air of grievance' and the 'cockiness that comes from being told too often that they and their city are special'.

All these people must now apologise – as of course must the *Sunday Times*, which on 28 February 1993 ran a huge feature by Jonathan Margolis under the headline 'SELF-PITY CITY'. After watching lynch-mobs throwing rocks at police vans containing the two boys accused of murdering James Bulger, Margolis denounced the city as a 'paranoia theme park' with a 'self-pitying and incipiently barbaric culture'.

But what do Liverpudlians themselves think of it? On 16 October the *Liverpool Daily Post* published an open letter to Boris Johnson from its editor, Jane Wolstenholme, attacking his 'outdated, breathtakingly unfair [and] just plain unpleasant' comments about Scousers. 'I do not recognise any "flawed psychological state" in the people of Liverpool,' she declared. 'Contrary to the image you present of paranoid, self-pitying and defeated people, the Liverpudlians I meet are self-confident, optimistic, proud of their heritage and looking forward with enthusiasm to a more prosperous future.'

So Wolstenholme would presumably have no truck with someone who called Liverpool a 'whingeing' city. This is the word used only last month by none other than Sir David Henshaw, the chief executive of Liverpool City Council. At a conference marketing Liverpool as the 2008 European city of culture, he admitted that 'sometimes it can still be the most mind-bogglingly awful and whingeing place, where the glass is always half-empty'.

Was Henshaw forced to march through the streets in sackcloth and ashes? Not at all. An editorial in Wolstenholme's *Daily Post* on 15 September praised the 'disarming candour' with which he had spoken: 'Sir David has aired opinions which may leave some people feeling slighted, even wounded. But if it goads them into action, not one word has been spoken out of place.'

Hacks and politicians should take note. Say that Scousers have a peculiar psyche and you'll never hear the end of it. Call them mind-bogglingly awful, however, and even the *Liverpool Daily Post* will congratulate you. As long as you're a Scouser, of course.

Hugh Shimmin 1862

How bitterly cold it is! How keenly the wind swirls through the narrow court! There are no sounds of revelry there now. Doors are shut, windows are stuffed. Here and there a shimmering gleam lights up a snow-rimed window sill. An hour ago, mother and children crouched around the small fire, and footsteps were eagerly listened for. It is Saturday night. Father is expected home with the wages. The remains of the thin candle have sunk in the socket of the iron holder.

It is no use applying at 'the little shop' for anything more now; as 'a clean book' cannot be shown. The children, wearied out, fall asleep. Mother throws over them what rags she can muster, and taking her youngest child to her bosom, and covering it as she best can with her tattered shawl, she steals out, gently drawing the door after her, and is now off in search of her husband.

From four houses out of six in this court, on this night, *seven* wives have gone to look for their husbands. The men are shipsmiths. In two instances, for months at a stretch, the weekly earnings of these men amounted to *ninety shillings*! – yes, often have they drawn five pounds a week; and yet they had scarcely a decent article of furniture in their houses, and nothing worthy the name of a bed to lie down upon.

Would you know how this state of things came to pass? Would you cease to theorise for a time, and *stoop* to look at facts? Follow then one of these wives; keep close up with her as she hurries along. Stand behind her as she pushes open the gin-palace door, by pressing the body of her babe against it! Look there! look there at the bright lights, the costly decorations, the beaming visages behind the bar, the steaming mixtures which are handed to the jabbering crowd, and think of the dark court, the dull misery-stricken house; the wife lean and vixenish, the children pallid and ragged. Can you see any connection between these?

One brazen door after another is pushed open – no husband is met with. Crossing Scotland-place you hear this: 'Haven't you found him? I found my chap, and good-humoured enough he was, too, for once. I got more than I expected from him; come and have two pennoth.' With compressed lips, from which bitter curses have just issued, muttering wrathful imprecations, and threatening vengeance, is it surprising that the shipsmith's wife yields to the solicitation of her neighbour? They go to have 'two pennoth'; and in this locality, as in many others, they have not far to go in order to reach a gin shop. Oh! what thanks are due to the magistrates for the kindness and consideration shown in providing these refreshment houses for their humble brethren! Oh! what paeans of praise will flow forth from wives driven to desperation, and children driven to crime, in consequence of the facilities afforded to their protectors for dallying with this body- and soul-destroying vice!

'Have a glass, Mary, have a glass; two pennoth is right enough when you can't get more, but have a *glass* now, it'll do you good this cold night. Dick, two glasses of whiskey.'

The young man thus familiarly addressed smilingly complies with the request, and the women toss off the drink before one can see who surrounds them. They have a good deal of talk before they think of going further, and their threats of vengeance are hurled about. At the door they meet a tall, swarthy man, whom they recognise, and elicit from him, after much to do, as the creature is far gone in drink, that 'Bill is tossing for quarts of ale at ____.' Away the women go. It is not far off, come along with them.

At the door of every gin shop which had been passed, stood puny young shivering children, in filth and tatters. 'Please give me a 'apenny', or 'please buy a box of matches', uttered in a drawl, first called attention to these sorrowful and pitiful objects. And no one who felt the weight, worth and influence of home – no one who gazed on the blear eyes, wan faces and stunted forms of children driven by parents to wear out their lives in such a manner – no one who had not torn off rudely the tender silken cords of a mother's love, which had been twined round the heart in infancy and childhood, and even yet, in vigorous manhood, vibrate when touched – no man, with right conceptions of the duties, obligations, responsibilities and hopes of life, could witness such scenes without fully endorsing the burning words of Charles Dickens:- 'There is not one of these – not one – but sows a harvest which mankind *must* reap. Open and unpunished murder in a city's streets would be less guilty in its daily toleration than one such spectacle as this.'

Alexei Sayle   1961

Mary, her mum and her dad lived in Anfield, North End of Liverpool. Valley Road off Oakfield Road, ten terraced streets along from Liverpool Football Club's ground. On Saturdays the Corporation parked all the special buses for the match in their road and the kids made sixpence by storing men's bikes in their backyards. Liverpool Football Club were hoping to get promoted from the second division but Mary's dad said it would never happen. Mary's family were Catholics so they automatically supported Everton but anybody who wanted to be associated with success and elegant football would have backed Everton anyway because they were much the better team, lording it over the top of the first division, their ground Goodison Park rising high above Stanley Park.

All the houses in Valley Road were made of the same neat yellow brick and every day all the wives used to get down on their hands and knees and scrub their doorsteps with a stone to redden them. All the children played in the street and roamed far beyond in huge packs, riding buses and trains and ferries. If the kids went to Stanley Park, the ornate, verdant fields dotted with gothic sandstone park shelters, which separated Anfield from the mighty Everton ground, they would be watched over and handed from one network of appointed and self-appointed guardians to another, like a jetliner leaving the air traffic controllers of one country and entering another's. Any minor mischief the kids might want to commit had to evade the attention of the cocky park watchmen, the park police, various freelance old enforcers and, worst of all, spies, narks and finks within their own organisation.

Nelly Weeton
1809

I had a beautiful sight today, of near a hundred sail, most of them going out, many of them very large vessels. If so many can go out at once, surely Liverpool cannot be so very greatly injured by the abolition of the slave trade.

Harriet Beecher Stowe
1853

Our carriage at last drove on, taking us through Liverpool; and a mile or two out, and at length wound its way along the gravel paths of a beautiful little retreat, on the banks of the Mersey, called the 'Dingle'. It opened to my eyes like a paradise, all wearied as I was with the tossing of the sea. I have since become familiar with these beautiful little spots, which are so common in England; but now all was entirely new to me.

We rode by shining clumps of the Portugal laurel, a beautiful evergreen, much resembling our mountain rhododendron; then there was the prickly, polished, dark-green holly, which I had never seen before, but which is, certainly, one of the most perfect of shrubs. The turf was of that soft, dazzling green, and had that peculiar velvet-like smoothness, which seem characteristic of England. We stopped at last before the door of a cottage, whose porch was overgrown with ivy. From that moment I ceased to feel myself a stranger in England. I cannot tell you how delightful to me, dizzy and weary as I was, was the first sight of the chamber of reception which had been prepared for us. No item of cozy comfort that one could desire was omitted. The sofa and easy chair wheeled up before a cheerful coal fire, a bright little teakettle steaming in front of the grate, a table with a beautiful vase of flowers, books, and writing apparatus, and kind friends with words full of affectionate cheer, – all these made me feel at home in a moment.

John Masefield 1931

A Liverpool Cathedral should be readily seen from many parts of the city, and, above all, by the life of the city, the river, with its ships and docks. All Cathedrals should be specially conspicuous by tower or spire, and these again should be made more conspicuous by some great figure of white or gold, the guardian of the city; and some further glory of windvanes, telling the windshifts, and great bells telling the hours and their quarters, and ringing for the city's joys; in this city, for the ship launched, or the ship come home...

BIOGRAPHIES

Lynette ARDEN (b 1943) is an Australian photographer now living in Adelaide who took photographs of Liverpool, and particularly Toxteth, where she lived for several years in the early 1970s.

Matthew ARNOLD (1822-1888) was a poet, writer and schools inspector who gave his 'Liverpool Address' at St George's Hall in 1882; he died on Park Road while rushing for a tram.

John James AUDUBON (1785-1851) was a Haitian artist who came to Liverpool in 1826 to raise funds for his mighty book *Birds of America*, of which Liverpool Central Library has a rare copy.

Dame Beryl BAINBRIDGE (b 1934) is a Lancashire-born novelist with more than twenty books to her name, some of which draw on her knowledge of Liverpool and time as an actress at the city's Playhouse Theatre.

Isabella BLOW (1958-2007) was a magazine editor from Cheshire who ran a feature in Tatler in 2002 on Liverpool fashion, dubbing the city 'Livercool'.

Johann Georg BODMER (1786-1864) was a Swiss engineer and inventor whose published diaries record a visit to

Liverpool in 1816 while touring British factories and leisure attractions.

Robert Carr BOSANQUET (1871-1935) was an esteemed archaeologist who was professor of classical archaeology at the University of Liverpool from 1906 until 1920.

John BROPHY (1899-1965) was a Liverpool-born writer who is little read nowadays but his once-popular novels include *Waterfront*, filmed in 1950 at the Liverpool docks.

William Cullen BRYANT (1794-1878) was an American Romantic poet and a founder of the Republican Party who arrived in Liverpool in 1845 at the start of a grand tour of Europe.

Josephine BUTLER (1828-1906) arrived in Liverpool with her husband in 1865, grieving for her six-year old daughter, and began a tireless campaign to help women in dire straits, especially prostitutes.

Margi CLARKE (b 1954) is an actress and TV presenter from Kirkby who starred in the film *Letter to Brezhnev*, set in 1980s Liverpool; she also runs a natural bodycare products company.

Christopher COLBECK (1809-1838) was a pianoforte maker in London who started his journal aged 11 and described a thoroughly modern trip to Liverpool by train in 1831.

Samuel Taylor COLERIDGE (1772-1834) was a Romantic poet who 'spent a very pleasant week' in Liverpool in 1804 but moaned about 'the Lousy Liverpool, the worst coach on the road'.

John CORNELIUS (b 1949) is a sketch artist and writer who was born in Crosby but was living in Toxteth when he found himself caught up in the riots of 1981.

Samuel Sullivan COX (1824-1889) was a widely-travelled American congressman and prolific writer who sailed to Liverpool in 1851 on the early Cunard steamship *Asia*.

Thomas CREEVEY (1768-1838) was a shrewd observer of the upper classes through his amusing letters; born in School Lane, Liverpool he was rumoured to be the natural son of the first Earl of Sefton.

Charles DICKENS (1812-1870) was always warmly received in Liverpool, which he held 'second in his heart to London', when he visited for his wildly popular public lecture tours.

Frederick DOUGLASS (1818-1895) was born into slavery but escaped aged 20 and became one of America's most skilled anti-slavery speakers, visiting Liverpool early in his career as an abolitionist in 1845.

Bill DRUMMOND (b 1953) is a Scottish musician and producer probably best known for burning a million pounds, who was a key figure in Liverpool's post-punk music scene.

Dr William Henry DUNCAN (1805-1863) was born in Liverpool, became England's first medical officer for health in the city, and highlighted the link between poverty and disease.

Jean-Michel DUTENS (1765-1848) was a French engineer sent to England by his government to study English canals and docks, and in Liverpool drew plans of the machinery at Princes Dock.

Daniel Clarke EDDY (1823-1896) was a Baptist minister, popular author and supporter of the 'Know-Nothings', a political party of the 1850s depicted in the 2002 film *Gangs of New York*.

Ralph Waldo EMERSON (1803-1882) was one of America's foremost writers and thinkers, who took several trips to England on lecture tours, landing at Liverpool for the first time in 1832.

Tracey EMIN (b 1963) is one of Britain's best known living artists who chose Liverpool for her first piece of public art, *The Roman Standard*, a tiny bird on a pole, in 2005.

William ENFIELD (1741-1797) was a Unitarian minister and historian from Suffolk who became minister for Benn's Garden Chapel in Liverpool and later moved to the Cairo Street Chapel in Warrington.

Friedrich ENGELS (1820-1895) was sent from his native Germany to run his father's cotton factory in Manchester, and was radicalised by the poverty, later meeting Marx and co-writing the 1848 *Communist Manifesto*.

Kenny EVERETT (1944-1995) was a comedian born in Seaforth, north Liverpool, who started his career as a DJ on pirate radio stations, later creating his own zany TV show on the 'Beeb', a term he coined.

Otto FRISCH (1904-1979) was a Jewish scientist who fled his native Austria in 1933 for London, moving to Liverpool in 1940 to work on nuclear chain reactions, often during black-outs and air raids.

Hans GÁL (1890-1987) was an Austrian composer who fled Vienna for England in 1938, and was living in Edinburgh when he was sent as an 'enemy alien' to Huyton Internment Camp in May 1940.

George GARRETT (1896-1966) was born in Seacombe, stowed away, joined a workers' organisation in New York, returning radicalised to Liverpool to write about poverty and unemployment in the 1920s.

Howard GAYLE (b 1958) was Liverpool FC's first black player, joining the club in 1977 and making his first team debut in 1980; he is now committed to nurturing young footballing talent in the city.

William Ewart GLADSTONE (1809-1898) was born in Rodney Street, Liverpool into a religious family that also owned slave plantations, and became British Prime Minister no fewer than four times.

Nathaniel HAWTHORNE (1804-1864) was an American writer best known for *The Scarlett Letter*, who was US Consul to Liverpool from 1853-1857, living with his family in Rock Ferry on the Wirral.

Sir George HEAD (1782-1855) was a popular author who received a knighthood from William IV in 1831 and left an account of his 'jumbling journey' around England at the beginning of Victoria's reign.

George Henry HEFFNER (1848-1932) was a teacher from Pennsylvania who set sail for Liverpool from New York in 1876 for a five month sightseeing tour of England, Europe and Egypt.

Oliver Wendell HOLMES (1809-1894) was a highly successful American physician, poet and writer who landed at Liverpool on a European trip with his daughter in 1886.

Gerard Manley HOPKINS (1844-1889) was a poet and Jesuit priest sent to St Francis Xavier's parish in Liverpool, where he felt miserable, 'museless' and shocked by the poverty.

Shirley HUGHES (b 1927) is a children's author and illustrator who was born and brought up in Hoylake on the

Wirral, the daughter of Liverpool department store owner T J Hughes.

Rachel KEMPSON (1910-2003) was an actress and matriarch of the Redgrave acting dynasty, who met her husband Sir Michael Redgrave while performing at the Liverpool Playhouse in 1935.

Caroline KIRKLAND (1801-1864) was born into a literary New York family but moved with her husband to Michigan where she wrote about frontier life, making her mark as a writer and later travelling abroad.

Johann Georg KOHL (1808-1878) was a German geographer who visited Liverpool in 1844 to tour the docks and new industries, possibly to indulge in industrial espionage.

Sir Oliver LODGE (1851-1940) was professor of maths and physics at University College Liverpool where his work included important discoveries in telegraphy; he was also interested in spiritualism.

Edward LUCIE-SMITH (b 1933) is a poet, cultural commentator and art critic who edited the classic 1967 book on the Liverpool Poets, *The Liverpool Scene*.

John MASEFIELD (1878-1967) was the English Poet Laureate who immortalised the call of the sea in his poem *Sea Fever* and who joined the merchant marine training ship HMS *Conway* at Liverpool in 1891.

Ann MAURY (1803-1876) was the only daughter of Liverpool's first US Consul, a writer who was born and lived in Liverpool until 1831, later returning for the opening of the Albert Dock in 1846.

James MAURY (1746-1840) was appointed US Consul to Liverpool in 1790, holding the post for forty years and living with his family in Rodney Street until he was widowed, after which he returned to America.

Roger McGOUGH (b 1937) is a radio presenter and well-loved performance poet who came to prominence in 1967 with the Liverpool poetry collection *The Mersey Sound*.

George MELLY (b 1926) has led an unconventional life variously as art collector, TV critic, jazz singer, Surrealist and fisherman but was born into a respectable and well-connected Liverpool family.

Herman MELVILLE (1819-1891) was the American author of *Moby Dick*, first sailed to Liverpool as a cabin boy in 1839, and used the experience for his early novel *Redburn*.

Paul MORLEY (b 1957) is a music journalist from Stockport who started his writing career on the *New Musical Express* and later promoted the Liverpool band Frankie Goes to Hollywood.

Charles NEVIN (b 1951) is a Fleet Street journalist, humorist, columnist and travel writer born in Liverpool to a Lancashire father and London mother, though he grew up in St Helens.

John NEWTON (1725-1807) was a Liverpool slave trader whose spiritual journey exceeded all his seafaring when he experienced a religious conversion, became a clergyman and wrote the hymn *Amazing Grace*.

George ORWELL (1903-1950) wrote *Animal Farm* and *Nineteen Eighty-Four* and tramped around England in his size eleven boots, visiting Liverpool in 1936 while researching *The Road to Wigan Pier*.

Dean Edward PATEY (1915-2005) was the Anglican Dean of Liverpool from 1964 to 1982 who oversaw the completion of Liverpool Cathedral and became a popular church leader.

Thomas PATTEN (1662-1726) was a wealthy Warrington merchant who made the River Mersey navigable from Runcorn to his copper-smelting works at Bank Quay in the late seventeenth century.

Sir Nikolaus PEVSNER (1902-1983) was a German Jewish refugee interned briefly at Huyton Internment Camp and later writing the groundbreaking *Buildings of England* architectural guides, including *South Lancashire* in 1969.

John Boynton PRIESTLEY (1894-1984) was a Bradford-born writer and founder member of CND whose travel writing from the 1930s, including a long passage about

Liverpool, voices his social concerns.

PRIVATE EYE is a satirical weekly magazine launched in 1961 by a group of school and university friends who all went on to have successful careers as comics and writers.

Eleanor RATHBONE (1872-1946) was a social activist and inveterate smoker who carried on the Rathbone philanthropic tradition in Liverpool, particularly championing women and families.

Julius RODENBERG (1831-1914) was a German writer and journalist who toured Wales in 1856, via Liverpool, and published a charming early account of Welsh history, folklore and customs.

Willy RUSSELL (b 1947) was born in Whiston near Liverpool and became a hairdresser but is now a celebrated Liverpool playwright, as well as a songwriter and novelist.

Siegfried SASSOON (1886-1967) was a writer and poet politicised by his experiences in the first world war; he was said to have thrown his Military Cross into the River Mersey but the medal turned up in an attic in May 2007.

Alexei SAYLE (b 1952) is an Anfield-born actor and comedian-turned-writer who started out as compere of the Comedy Store in London and starred in the 1980s cult comedy *The Young Ones*.

Johanna SCHOPENHAUER (1766-1838) was a writer born in Danzig, now Gdansk, who visited Liverpool in 1803, and was the estranged mother of philosopher Arthur Schopenhauer.

Walter Dixon SCOTT (1881-1915) was born in Kirkdale, Liverpool and was a talented writer whose life was cut short by dysentery contracted at the first world war battle of Gallipoli.

Will SELF (b 1961) is a journalist and novelist who stayed on the twenty first floor of a half-empty tower block on Liverpool's Sheil Road in 2003, before it was demolished, writing about the experience.

Right Reverend Lord David SHEPPARD (1929-2005) was a cricketer and Bishop of Liverpool from 1975 to 1997, and wrote the influential *Faith in the City* report on inner city poverty in 1985.

Hugh SHIMMIN (1819-1879) moved to Liverpool from the Isle of Man and became an acid-penned journalist, chronicling the social and moral ills of all classes of Liverpool society.

Samuel SIDNEY (1813-1883) had a varied career including a stint as a lawyer in Liverpool but is best known as a writer on railways, including a tour to Liverpool in his 1851 *Rides on Railways*.

Margaret SIMEY (1906-2004) was a social reformer who

came to Liverpool from Glasgow aged 18, and spent the rest of her long life championing the city's less well off, particularly in Toxteth.

James STONEHOUSE (c1809-1890) wrote memoirs of Liverpool life, reputedly as a local nonagenarian; in reality he was born in London, moved to Liverpool as a boy and remained until his death aged 81.

Harriet Beecher STOWE (1811-1896) was an American abolitionist who sailed to Liverpool in 1853 for a European tour for her book *Uncle Tom's Cabin* and the evils of slavery.

Jack STRAW (b 1946) is a former Labour Home Secretary who made his unfortunate comment about Liverpudlians at a meeting in Milton Keynes, then went on local radio to atone.

Henry STRIPE (1813-1899) arrived in Liverpool in 1832 to try his luck as a 'pushing young man' and joined the metals business of shipowners John Bibby & Sons; he worked as a clerk for 46 years.

Hyppolite TAINE (1828-1893) was a prominent French intellectual, an influential historian, philosopher and sociologist who visited Liverpool in 1871, later publishing his descriptions as *Notes sur l'Angleterre*.

Margaret THATCHER (b 1925) is a former Conservative Prime Minister of Britain who condoned the first English use of CS gas in Liverpool during the Toxteth riots in 1981.

Barry UNSWORTH (b 1930) is an English novelist and former writer in residence at the University of Liverpool who used the city's slave-trading past in his novel *Sacred Hunger*, winner of the 1992 Booker Prize.

Dirk Pieter VAN DEN BERGH (1864-1933) emigrated in 1906 from Holland to Canada with his wife Elske and nine children, writing in his diary about the stressful eight days' wait for a ship in Liverpool.

Nelly WEETON (1776-1849) was a governess born in Lancaster who also lived (and died) in Liverpool and whose journals reveal a stoicism in the face of hardship and betrayal.

Reverend John WESLEY (1703-1791) was a theologian, abolitionist and leader of the Methodist movement who preached extensively around the country, making several trips to Liverpool.

BOOK LIST

Matthew ARNOLD: *A Liverpool Address on the Opening of the Session of University College, Liverpool, 1882*, from *Five Uncollected Essays of Matthew Arnold* (Liverpool Reprints Number 9) ed Kenneth Allott, Liverpool, University Press of Liverpool, 1953

John James AUDUBON: *The 1826 Journal of John James Audubon* ed Alice Ford, University of Oklahoma Press, 1967

Beryl BAINBRIDGE: *The Dressmaker*, Gerald Duckworth & Co, 1973

Johann Georg BODMER: *Industrial Britain under the Regency, The Diaries of Escher, Bodmin, May & de Gallois, 1816*, ed William Otto Henderson, Cass, 1968

Robert Carr BOSANQUET: *Letters and Light Verse*, ed Ellen Sophia Bosanquet, John Bellows, Gloucester, 1938

John BROPHY: *City of Departures*, Collins, 1946

William Cullen BRYANT: *Letters of a Traveller; or, Notes of Things Seen in Europe and America*, 1850

Josephine BUTLER: *Josephine Butler, An Autobiographical Memoir*, ed George William Johnson and Lucy Johnson, Arrowsmith, 1909

Christopher COLBECK: *The Journals of Christopher Colbeck, 1831*, unpublished typescript held at Merseyside Maritime

Museum Archives & Library

Samuel Taylor COLERIDGE, *Collected Letters of Samuel Taylor Coleridge,* ed Earl Leslie Griggs Vol III 1807-1814, Oxford: Clarendon Press, 1959

John CORNELIUS: *Liverpool 8*, Liverpool University Press, 1982

Samuel Sullivan COX: *A Buckeye Abroad; or, Wanderings in Europe, and in the Orient*, 1851

Thomas CREEVEY: *The Creevey Papers*, ed Sir Herbert Eustace Maxwell, Murray, 1904

Charles DICKENS, *Poor Mercantile Jack*, from *The Uncommercial Traveller*, 1860

Frederick DOUGLASS: *My Bondage and My Freedom*, 1855

Bill DRUMMOND: *45*, Little, Brown, 2000

Dr William Henry DUNCAN, *The Sanitary Condition of the Labouring Population of England*, Local Reports, 1842

Jean-Michel DUTENS: *Memoires sur les Travaux Publics d'Angleterre, 2 Vols, Paris, 1819, Vol 2* from *Foul Berths and French Spies*, Adrian Jarvis, National Museums Liverpool, 2003

Daniel Clarke EDDY: *Europa: or, Scenes and Society in England, France, Italy and Switzerland*, 1859

Ralph Waldo EMERSON: *English Traits*, 1856

Tracey EMIN: *My Life in a Column*, The Independent, 7

April, 2006

William ENFIELD: *Essay towards the history of Leverpool*, Joseph Johnson, 1774

Friedrich ENGELS: *Condition of the Working Class in England, 1845*, London, 1891

Kenny EVERETT: *The Custard Stops at Hatfield*, Willow, 1982

Otto FRISCH, *What Little I Remember*, Cambridge University Press, 1979

Hans GÁL: *Music Behind Barbed Wire, A diary of the summer of 1940*, Peter Lang, 2003, ed Eva Fox-Gál, trs Eva Fox-Gál, 2007

George GARRETT: *The Pianist*, from *The Collected George Garrett*, Trent Editions, 1999

William Ewart GLADSTONE: from *The Life of William Ewart Gladstone, Vol 1 (1808-1859)*, John Morley, MacMillan & Co, 1903

Nathaniel HAWTHORNE: *English Notebooks*, Kegan Paul, 1883

Sir George HEAD: *A Home Tour through the Manufacturing Districts of England, Summer 1835*, Cass, 1968

George Henry HEFFNER: *The Youthful Wanderer, or An Account of a Tour through England, France, Belgium, Holland, Germany and the Rhine, Switzerland, Italy, and Egypt, Adapted to the Wants of Young Americans Taking Their First*

Glimpses at the Old World, 1876

Oliver Wendell HOLMES: *Our Hundred Days in Europe*, 1887

Gerard Manley HOPKINS: from a letter to Robert Bridges, *Gerard Manley Hopkins Selected Prose*, Oxford University Press, 1980

Shirley HUGHES: *A Life Drawing*, Bodley Head, 2002

Rachel KEMPSON: *A Family and its Fortunes*, Gerald Duckworth & Co, 1986

Caroline KIRKLAND: *Holidays Abroad; Or, Europe from the West*, 1849

Johann Georg KOHL: *In England and Wales, 1844*, Cass, 1968

Oliver LODGE: *Past Years*, Hodder & Stoughton, 1931

Edward LUCIE-SMITH: *The Liverpool Scene*, Donald Carroll, 1967

John MASEFIELD: *The Conway*, Heinemann, 1933

Ann and James MAURY: extracts from *Intimate Virginiana, a Century of Maury Travels by Land and Sea*, ed Anne Fontaine Maury, The Dietz Press, 1941

George MELLY: *Scouse Mouse*, Weidenfeld & Nicolson, 1984

Herman MELVILLE: *Redburn, His first voyage*, 1849

Paul MORLEY: *Liverpool Surreal* from *Centre of the Creative*

Universe: Liverpool and the Avant Garde, ed Christoph Grunenberg, Liverpool University Press, 2007

Charles NEVIN: *Scouse Dreams*, from *Lancashire, Where Women Die of Love*, Mainstream, 2004

John NEWTON: letter to his wife, from *History of the Liverpool Privateers and Letters of Marque, with an account of the Liverpool Slave Trade 1744-1812*, Gomer Williams, Heinemann, 1897

George ORWELL: *The Road to Wigan Pier Diary* from *The Collected Essays, Journalism, and Letters of George Orwell, Volume 1: An Age Like This, 1920-1940* ed Sonia Orwell and Ian Angus, David Godine, 2000

Edward PATEY: from *Today's Cathedral*, Joe Riley, SPCK, 1978

Thomas PATTEN: from a letter to Richard Norris of Speke Hall, 1697, original held at Liverpool Record Office

Nikolaus PEVSNER: *The Buildings of England, South Lancashire*, Penguin, 1969

J B PRIESTLEY: *English Journey*, Heinemann, 1934

PRIVATE EYE: *Beyond the Whinge,* Hackwatch, Private Eye, 29 October 2004

Eleanor RATHBONE: *William Rathbone, A Memoir*, MacMillan & Co, 1905

Julius RODENBERG: *An Autumn in Wales (1856), Country and People, Tales and Songs*, trs and ed William Linnard, D Brown and Sons, 1985

Willy RUSSELL: from *Liverpool: the First 1,000 Years*, Arabella McIntyre-Brown, Garlic Press, 2001

Siegfried SASSOON: *Memoirs of an Infantry Officer*, Faber & Faber, 1930

Alexei SAYLE: *The Last Woman Killed in the War*, from *Barcelona Plates*, Hodder & Stoughton, 2000

Johanna SCHOPENHAUER: *A Lady Travels, Journeys in Scotland and England*, 1803, trs Mariane Della Rocca, 2007

Walter Dixon SCOTT: *Liverpool 1907*, A & C Black, 1907

Will SELF: *Mersey Mersey Me, Psychogeography 5*, The Independent, 1 October, 2003

David SHEPPARD: *Steps along Hope Street, My Life in London and Liverpool*, Hodder & Stoughton, 2002

Hugh SHIMMIN: *An Hour in a Grog Shop*, Liverpool Sketches, 1863

Samuel SIDNEY: *Rides on Railways*, 1851

James STONEHOUSE: *Recollections of Old Liverpool, by a nonagenarian*, J F Hughes, 1863

Harriet Beecher STOWE: *Sunny Memories of Foreign Lands*, Sampson Low, 1854

Henry STRIPE: *Sketch of the Commercial Life of H E Stripe*, unpublished diary held at Merseyside Maritime Museum Archives & Library, DX/1477

Hyppolite TAINE: *Notes on England*, W Isbister & Co, 1874

Margaret THATCHER: *House of Commons Parliamentary Questions*, Hansard, 9 July, 1981

Barry UNSWORTH: *Sacred Hunger*, Hamish Hamilton, 1991

Dirk Pieter VAN DEN BERGH: unpublished diary held at Merseyside Maritime Museum Archives & Library, SAS/3/1/16

Nelly WEETON: *Journal of a Governess Vol 1, 1807-1811*, ed Edward Hall, Oxford University Press, 1936

John WESLEY: *The Journal of the Reverend John Wesley*, ed Nehemiah Curnock, Epworth Press, 1911-1916

ACKNOWLEDGEMENTS

Lynette Arden: by kind permission of 800 Lives Contemporary Collecting Project, Museum of Liverpool, National Museums Liverpool

John James Audubon, *The 1826 Journal of John James Audubon*: reproduced by kind permission of the Estate of Alice Elizabeth Ford

Beryl Bainbridge: *The Dressmaker*, Gerald Duckworth & Co Ltd, 1973, © Beryl Bainbridge 1973

Isabella Blow: reprinted by kind permission of Tatler

Johann Georg Bodmer, *Industrial Britain under the Regency, The Diaries of Escher, Bodmin, May & de Gallois*, reproduced by kind permission of Frank Cass

Robert Carr Bosanquet, *Letters and Light Verse*: reproduced by kind permission of the Bosanquet family

John Brophy, *City of Departures*: © The Estate of John Brophy

Margi Clarke, *Liverpool City*, Issue 6: by kind permission of Liverpool City Council

Christopher Colbeck, *The Journals of Christopher Colbeck, 1831*: by kind permission of Joyce Colbeck Robinson and family

Samuel Tayor Coleridge, *Collected Letters of Samuel Taylor Coleridge*: reproduced by kind permission of Oxford University Press

John Cornelius, *Liverpool 8*: reproduced by kind permission of Liverpool University Press.

Samuel Sullivan Cox, *A Buckeye Abroad*: Rare Books and Manuscripts Library, Ohio State University

Bill Drummond, *45* (2000): reproduced by kind permission of Little, Brown

Jean-Michel Dutens, *Memoires sur les Travaux Publics d'Angleterre, Paris 1819*: reproduced by kind permission of The Institution of Civil Engineers.

Tracey Emin, *My Life in a Column*: © Tracey Emin, 2006

Kenny Everett, *The Custard Stops at Hatfield*: Arrow 1983 (first published by Willow, 1982), by kind permission of Lennard Associates Ltd

Otto Frisch, *What Little I Remember*: reproduced by kind permission of Cambridge University Press

Hans Gál, *Musik hinter Stacheldraht*: Eva Fox-Gál, (Hrsg.) Bern: Peter Lang, 2003

George Garrett, *The Pianist; The Collected George Garrett*, Ed. Michael Murphy: reproduced by kind permission of Trent Editions

Howard Gayle: by kind permission of Howard Gayle

Gerard Manley Hopkins, from a letter to Robert Bridges, *Gerard Manley Hopkins Selected Prose*: for works in copyright by Permission of Oxford University Press on behalf of The British Province of the Society of Jesus

Shirley Hughes, *A Life Drawing*: published by the Bodley Head. Reprinted by permission of the Random House Group Ltd

Rachel Kempson, *A family and its fortunes (1986)*: reproduced by kind permission of Gerald Duckworth & Co Ltd

J G Kohl, *In England & Wales*: reproduced by kind permission of Frank Cass

Oliver Lodge, *Past Years*: by kind permission of Oliver R W W Lodge

Edward Lucie-Smith, *The Liverpool Scene*: © Edward Lucie-Smith; first published by Donald Carroll (1967)

John Masefield, *The Conway*: reprinted by kind permission of the Society of Authors as the Literary Representative of the Estate of John Masefield

Ann and James Maury, extracts from *Intimate Virginiana, a Century of Maury Travels by Land and Sea*: by kind permission of the Fontaine Maury Society

Roger McGough, *Liverpool City*, Issue 9: by kind permisison of

Liverpool City Council

George Melly, *Scouse Mouse*: reproduced by kind permission of Weidenfeld & Nicolson, a division of the Orion Publishing Group

Paul Morley, *Liverpool Surreal*, from *Centre of the Creative Universe: Liverpool and the Avant Garde*, ed Christoph Grunenberg, © Paul Morley 2007: by kind permission of Paul Morley

Charles Nevin, *Lancashire: Where Women Die of Love* (2004): reprinted courtesy of Mainstream Publishing

George Orwell, *The Road To Wigan Pier* by George Orwell (Copyright © George Orwell, 1937): by permission of Bill Hamilton as the Literary Executor of the Estate of the Late Sonia Brownell Orwell and Secker & Warburg Ltd

Edward Patey, *Today's Cathedral*: by kind permission of Joe Riley

Nikolaus Pevsner, *South Lancashire* (Penguin Books, 1969): copyright © Nikolaus Pevsner 1969

J B Priestley, *English Journey*: Extracts from *English Journey*: (Copyright © Estate of J.B.Priestley 1934) by J.B. Priestley are reproduced by permission of PFD (www.pfd.co.uk) on behalf of the Estate of J.B. Priestley

Private Eye, *Hackwatch*, Issue 1118, p.5: Reproduced by kind permission of PRIVATE EYE www.private-eye.co.uk

Julius Rodenberg, *An Autumn in Wales (1856), Country and People,*

ILLUSTRATIONS

These striking illustrations were commissioned for Mersey Minis from artist Clare Curtis, and present her unique visual response to Liverpool. Clare follows a long tradition of British printmakers with her distinctive linocuts, which are imbued with a bold, contemporary feel. Felixstowe-based Clare demonstrates her empathy with the sea with maritime patterns and motifs appearing throughout her work.

These specially commissioned icons have been chosen for their multi-layered local references.

Front door: Georgian doors, with their distinctive fanlights, can still be seen in areas of Liverpool such as Everton, Canning, and Ropewalks. These were the homes of Liverpool's 18th century merchants.

Palm House: The Sefton Park Palm House was opened in 1896 by Queen Victoria. Smashed first by the Blitz in 1941, then later by neglect, it was restored to its former splendour and reopened in 2001.

Steam train: Stephenson won the Rainhill Trials with *Rocket* in 1829, for the world's first passenger railway line (Liverpool to Manchester); classic toys Hornby Trains and Meccano were invented in Liverpool.

Cotton: Bound up with the city's fortunes – cotton picked by slaves transported by Liverpool ships, trade links with India and Egypt; even today 70% of world cotton for export is sold under Liverpool arbitration.

Music: Liverpool boasts world-class music from sea shanties to the Royal Liverpool Philharmonic; Merseybeat hit international consciousness in the 1960s, but owes its heritage to cultures from around the world.

Neptune: Roman God of the Sea, mythical feature on the city coat of arms; the planet Neptune was the final home of the highly evolved human race in local writer Olaf Stapledon's *Last and First Men*.

Oak leaves: Quintessentially English; the Allerton Oak (over 1,000 years old); timber exports from Liverpool; the district of Aigburth means 'grove of oaks'; oak timbers were used to build ships on the Mersey.

THE EDITOR

Though a land-lubber herself, Deborah Mulhearn was born in Liverpool into a family with a typically seafaring tradition.

She left school at 16 and worked in the wardrobe department of the Liverpool Playhouse. She then went back to formal education, studying English Literature at the University of Liverpool.

After the requisite stint in London, where she worked for five years in publishing and as a journalist on the Architects' Journal, she returned to Liverpool in 1991 to pursue a freelance career in journalism. She writes for a wide variety of newspapers and magazines and has contributed to several books on architecture, history and environment.

THANKS

I'd like to thank the following people who have helped shape LIVING in different ways, supplying books, names, dates, details; ideas, support, advice, ears, eyes and enthusiasm: Michael Bailey; Damien Bicknell, Andrew Brown; Eva Fox-Gál; Paul Gallagher, Museum of Liverpool Life; Dr David Gill; David & Carolyn Irvine; Karen Kilcup, University of North Carolina; Haile McCollum; Brenda Murray; Joseph Peters; Dr Peter Rowlands, University of Liverpool; David & Deborah Singmaster; Adam Turner; Beccy Turner, The Wordsworth Trust; Beth Staunton; Ron Stewart; H Lewis Ulman, Ohio State University; Roger Hull and staff at Liverpool archives and local studies, Liverpool Libraries; Andy Sawyer and staff at Special Collections and Archives, Sydney Jones Library, University of Liverpool, and many more librarians, biographers, publishers, archivists and curators in and beyond Liverpool.

Very grateful thanks to Rachel Mulhearn, Adrian Jarvis and Mary Earnshaw from whose ideas Mersey Minis evolved; to Pauline McAdam and BBC Radio Merseyside for their valued support of Mersey Minis; and to Arabella and Fiona at Capsica who saw the potential to create a wonderful literary keepsake for Liverpool, and then went on and created it.

INDEX OF AUTHORS

MERSEY MINIS

LIVING is the second of five volumes in the Mersey Minis series, published during 2007, Liverpool's 800th anniversary year. Four volumes – LANDING, LIVING, LOVING, LEAVING – are collections of writing from the past eight centuries. The third volume in the series, LONGING, will contain entirely new writing from around the world, marking a beat in Liverpool's remarkable history.

To find out more about the Mersey Minis series, log on to www.merseyminis.com

CAPSICA

Capsica is an independent publishing house based in Liverpool, specialising in high quality non-fiction. If you have enjoyed LIVING, you might like to read some of our other publications. You can read about the books on their blogs, and buy on www.loveliverpoolbooks.com.

http://napkinfolding.blogspot.com/
http://liverpoolfirst1000years.blogspot.com
http://cultureofcapital.blogspot.com/